A POCKET GUIDE

THE

PLACE-NAMES OF WALES

A POCKET GUIDE

THE
PLACE-NAMES
OF WALES

HYWEL WYN OWEN

UNIVERSITY OF WALES PRESS
THE WESTERN MAIL
1998

© Hywel Wyn Owen, 1998

First published by the University of Wales Press and The Western Mail 1998
Reprinted 2000
Reprinted by the University of Wales Press 2005

ISBN 0-7083-1458-9

A catalogue record for this book is available from the British Library

The front cover shows a map by John Speed (1610)
(with the permission of Llyfrgell Genedlaethol Cymru/The National Library of
Wales)

Original cover design by Chris Neale
Typeset in Wales at the University of Wales Press
Printed in Malta by Gutenberg Press

Contents

Acknowledgements

This book was prompted by an invitation from Ned Thomas, Director of the University of Wales Press, to consider writing a selective reference book on the place-names of Wales. His encouragement, together with the diligence and support of Susan Jenkins, Senior Editor, have made a difficult task a very satisfying one.

I have been privileged for many years to have access to Professor Melville Richards's vast corpus of research material at the University of Wales Bangor. The curator of that archive, Tomos Roberts, and another good friend, Emeritus Professor Gwynedd O. Pierce, both provided invaluable help from their own unrivalled knowledge of place-names in Wales.

My conscience dictates that I declare my appreciation of my wife's remarkable patience in sharing a summer holiday with this book. My daughter assisted in preparing the text and accommodated countless emendations. I am grateful to both.

i gofio'r
Coleg Normal
1858–1996

Introduction

This is an accessible reference book for anyone wishing to learn about the place-names of Wales. The media and popular press provide ample evidence of a current surge of interest in the names that surround us. This reflects a greater awareness of our environment, an appreciation of the wealth of local history, and a more sophisticated response to the interplay of the Welsh and English languages.

A 'Pocket Guide' to the Place-names of Wales cannot include every place-name, and it does not say everything that could be said about each name. Its aim is to help to satisfy a demonstrable curiosity in place-names. Later in the Introduction there is a section explaining how the place-names were selected, and other sections show what the study of place-names involves and how names can reveal fascinating insights into the people, history, environment and language of places.

Place-names and language

It may sound like stating the obvious but studying place-names means studying the names of places; it is essentially a linguistic study. As well as telling us about the places themselves, place-names can tell us something about language.

Place-names can, for example, reveal the influence of one language upon another. There are a whole range of place-names in England with recognizable Welsh counterparts such as Dover (**dwfr** 'water'), Avon (**afon** 'river'), and Tarvin (**terfyn** 'boundary'). Similarly, there are a number of place-names in Wales which are English in origin but which have 'gone native' and acquired a Welsh spelling and pronunciation, for example Erddig 'herder's cottage' and Bagillt 'Bacca's lea'.

Such naturalized place-names in Wales can preserve a sound which has long since disappeared in standard English speech. Newborough on Anglesey is today pronounced in the same way as any borough in England, but the Welsh form Niwbwrch retains the **-ch** currently heard in Welsh **bach** and Scottish **loch** and which would have been heard in the medieval pronunciation of Newborough. This was a sound once commonly heard in English and usually spelt **-gh**. On the other hand, Dinbych and Denbigh illustrate the same point in reverse: Dinbych is the original Welsh form and Denbigh is the English spelling, where **-gh** represented **-ch**.

The spelling of a place-name will sometimes be at variance with the way in which we actually say it. Denbigh is regularly pronounced 'Dembigh' because in rapid speech **-nb-** will tend to become **-mb-**. The same is true of Llanbedr Pont Steffan which is both locally and nationally referred to as 'Llambed'; the spelling of the English form, Lampeter, has in fact kept up with the pronunciation. Harlech (**hardd-lech**) illustrates a common feature in place-names, the assimilation of sounds, as does Porthaethwy from **porth** and **Daethwy**. The preferences of pronunciation will sometimes alter the order of sounds, so that **rhoddni** became Rhondda.

We should not be so concerned with the sounds of place-names in this section that we forget their meaning. Place-names can preserve meanings which have long since disappeared or which are rapidly disappearing from everyday language. Take Bangor. A certain type of pleached hedge was called a **bangor** and laying such a hedge was called **bangori**, both words being restricted to agricultural practice in certain parts of Wales. Yet, the place-name deriving from **bangor** is one of the best-known place-names within Wales and beyond. Take Bala. The outlet of a river from a lake was called a **bala**, not a word in everyday use today, but most people are familiar with Bala, the outlet of the river Dee from Llyn Tegid, without being aware of the actual meaning.

Meanings can change too. The Old English word **tūn** (pronounced 'toon'), found as **-ton** at the end of names such as Norton, Weston, Sutton and Aston, originally meant 'farm' or 'enclosure' and only later developed into the word 'town' as we think of it today. It is also worth noting that in north-east Wales a number of **tūn** place-names were naturalized to forms such as Prestatyn, Mostyn and Estyn, whereas the standard English development was to Preston, Moston and Aston.

Place-names and history

In the preceding section we saw that studying place-names means studying the actual names. However, names may have significance within the historical context in which they were given initially or in which they subsequently developed. Indeed, place-names can frequently add to our knowledge of the history of places. Interestingly enough, place-names can sometimes be the only trace of otherwise unrecorded history. Some burial mounds have survived, but many have not (frequently because of human activity) and the place-name may be vital evidence for an archaeologist. Barrow in England is an obvious example as are Gwyddgrug and Yr Wyddgrug, 'the burial mound', in Wales.

In the previous section we also saw examples of place-names in England which have Welsh counterparts. Such names are living evidence that Brythonic, the antecedent of Welsh, was spoken in England. The Romans left their mark in the various **-chesters** and **-casters** scattered throughout England, and in Caerleon which incorporates the Latin word for 'legion'. In Wales, the Vikings can be traced in such Scandinavian names as Anglesey, Orme, Skomer and Swansea. The Norman Conquest gave rise to place-names like Montgomery and Beaumaris.

There are many place-names which record some aspect of medieval life, such as castles (Denbigh), prisons (Cricieth), market places (Chepstow), enclosure and hunting (Hay-on-Wye), religious practices (Holywell, Presteigne, Merthyr Tydfil), ferries (Porthaethwy), dykes and boundaries (Trefyclo), and settlements (Newport). Scores of people live on in place-names, some identifiable (Brecon, Trefaldwyn and the many saints commemorated in **llan** names); some are lost to us (Abertillery, Caerphilly) and others have become the stuff of legend (Caerfyrddin, Beddgelert).

More recent industrial history is better documented. Nevertheless, in time, as collieries and quarries close and docks become marinas, it may be that Tylorstown, Morriston and Porthmadog will be the only records of industrial entrepreneurs and their dependent communities. Fortunately, place-names do tend to have a resilient longevity.

Some historical events gave names to places. The battle commemorated in Battle Abbey and Battle is the one fought in Hastings 1066, while Battlefield refers to the Battle of Shrewsbury in 1403. The Crimea Pass (near Blaenau Ffestiniog) and the Waterloo Bridge (near Betws-y-Coed) both belong to later periods.

Names pertaining to religious sites also reflect the history of such settlements. Some, like Betws (itself an English word meaning 'bead-house', 'a house of prayer'), indicate a solitary cell; others, like Merthyr, denote the burial of a saint. Far more common is **llan**, originally 'enclosed land', then 'enclosed land for a cemetery around a church', then used of the church itself and finally associated with the parish. Most examples of **llan** commemorate the saint to whom the church is dedicated (such as Llandudno and Llanelli); others identify the location of the church (as in Llan-faes 'the church in open land', and Llangoed 'the church surrounded by or near trees', adjacent parishes in Anglesey).

Place-names and the landscape

It is likely that the most influential factor in determining the name of a place is its location or its relationship to the visible landscape. Some advantageous characteristic may have attracted settlers, perhaps the fertile land in a valley bottom or maybe the craggy outcrop of a defensible position. The view from a settlement may have inspired its name. Occasionally, if development has obliterated the feature which prompted the name, we have to imagine the original scene; cities and towns are particularly prone to losing their naming feature. Elsewhere we cannot be quite sure what the names actually meant, since at the end of the twentieth century we have lost the country-dweller's subtle distinctions in interpreting the landscape.

The prominent position of a place, whether viewed from afar or from the actual location (Pembroke, Penarth), is an obvious incentive. The hill may have on it a distinctive mound perhaps associated with fortification (Crickhowell) or burial (Yr Wyddgrug). The settlers' attention could have been drawn to the colour of the soil (Rhuddlan, Radnor), a topographic feature (Rhaeadr, Rhyl, Welshpool) or a feature in the course of a river (Abergele, Ammanford). In Wales, the sea and the coastline frequently contributed to the naming process (Pwllheli, Tywyn), especially when human activity was also involved (Fishguard, Newport, Porthcawl, Milford Haven). Inland, the reference may be to agricultural practice (Builth) or specific buildings (Bridgend, Pontypridd). Occasionally, we may find the place-name expressing simple admiration (Maes-teg, Harlech, Beaumaris).

The study of place-names

The foregoing sections have served to underline the careful detective work which goes into ascribing a meaning and significance to a place-name. It should be evident by now that the current form of a place-name may or may not be relied on as an accurate guide to the original name. Maes-teg is self-evident, as it happens, but Builth needs considerable dissection before we get anywhere. Take the names of four of the University seats of learning in Wales. Aberystwyth seems simple enough, since **aber** is common for a river or mouth of a river and there is a river Ystwyth there; however Aberystwyth is on the river Rheidol. It is possible to associate some form of the river-name Taff with Cardiff but how does that square with the Welsh form Caerdydd? Swansea has nothing to do with a swan or the sea. Bangor defies divination.

In these four instances we cannot begin any explanation without knowing what the place-names were like when they were first recorded. That could be fourteen centuries ago. Even the earliest record is not always reliable if the place and the place-name existed long before that, but it is the best we can do and, if we are to try to explain the origin of the name, it is the only thing we can do.

These early forms are to be found in a variety of sources, some contemporary, most later, encompassing monastic and ecclesiastical records, charters, legal documents, deeds, estate papers and surveys, chronicles, parish registers, tithe schedules, land tax and census returns and a whole host of maps which frequently accompany such records. Some source materials will be in published form, but many will require scrutiny of original documents; some will be in local archive offices, others will be in private hands or national collections. All in all, we need to have access to any document which records the names of places within a community. The gathering of place-name data is the first stage in the detective work.

The second stage is analysing this data. We must be alert to the possible transmission of recording errors as, say, where a thirteenth-century Norman-French civil-servant may have copied a Latin legal document compiled by an English land-lord based on evidence supplied by a Welsh tenant. Analysis, we have already seen, is primarily a linguistic task for which a knowledge of the history and development of the Welsh and English languages is essential, together with a working knowledge of elements from other languages which appear in the place-names of Wales, such as Latin, Old Norse and Norman-French. These elements provide place-name re-searchers with some of their most valuable tools. If a place-name's first recorded form can reliably be broken down into recognizable constituent elements from the common stock, then the meaning of those elements will already be known.

This brings us to the third stage, that of interpretation. Here we bring the study of place-names back to the location or the occasion which first initiated the naming. Wherever possible we must identify the place referred to and test the linguistic proposition against known history and the landscape as it probably was. If there appears to be a mismatch, questions must be asked. Can the earliest forms be trusted? Is the linguistic analysis correct? Has the landscape changed in any way? Did the name refer to a slightly different area from the one currently associated with the name? Does the current pronunciation provide an additional clue? This is the stage at which the study of place-names depends on geology, geography, industrial archaeology and so on. It is the stage at which the local historian has much to contribute.

All scholars studying place-names will adopt the rigorous methodology described in the preceding paragraphs. Most, if not all, of the major place-names in Britain will have been dealt with in this way, with the findings published in various journals and dictionaries of place-names. This is the selective approach. A more comprehensive and exhaustive approach is described as a place-name survey, a detailed study of all major and minor names in a specified area. Such a survey allows for a thorough coverage of all the place-names in the area, which not only adds considerably to the understanding of the area's language, history and landscape but also adds incrementally to the store of our knowledge of place-names in Britain, especially place-name elements.

Under the aegis of the English Place-Name Society the place-name survey approach has been successfully pursued county by county for over seventy years. In Wales, Scotland and Ireland progress at the county level has been more leisurely, but the separate national place-name associations have adopted broadly the same strategy as England.

In Wales, pioneering selective work has been accomplished over many years by a number of eminent individual scholars. Detailed surveys have been published for Dinas Powys, Pembrokeshire and East Flintshire. Various local and county societies are supporting research projects and publications, as is the Cambrian Archaeological Association, while the Place-Name Survey Committee of the University of Wales's Board of Celtic Studies is co-ordinating research funding. A book on the major place-names of Wales does therefore have authoritative sources at its disposal. One of the most influential is *The Names of Towns and Cities in Britain*, the Welsh material for which was written by Professor Melville Richards almost thirty years ago. Several subsequent dictionaries for Britain have drawn heavily on this material, and this book is no exception.

Place-names and the Welsh language

You need no knowledge of Welsh to follow the explanations of the origin, development and meaning of the place-names in this book. However, it would be as well to illustrate very briefly some of the ways in which place-names are formed in Welsh and highlight occasional sound changes peculiar to Welsh.

Very many Welsh place-names can be described as name-phrases, a structure also common to English place-names. For example, in English 'the new town' will eventually become Newtown, and in Welsh 'y dre newydd' (with the adjective following the noun in the usual way) will eventually give Y Drenewydd. Notice that in English and Welsh the name-phrase has come to be written as one word. If the single word has the conventional Welsh stress (the penultimate stress) on the appropriate syllable all is well, as in Llandrindod and Aberystwyth. If, however, the single word appears to invite a stress on an inappropriate syllable then it is customary to hyphenate the name-phrase. Two simple examples from adjoining parishes in Anglesey will illustrate the distinction: Llangoed is stressed on the penultimate (and therefore first) syllable; Llan-faes is stressed on the second syllable and is hyphenated to protect this stress on the more significant element in the name-phrase. However, it must be admitted that this convention is not always observed, and you are as likely to find Llanfaes as Llan-faes in writing; nevertheless whatever the written form, the pronunciation always stresses the second syllable. In a longer name-phrase, such as Betws-y-Coed, the written form reflects the stress which falls on the final **coed**; writing it as 'Betwsycoed' offends both eye and ear. To confound us all, a number of place-names have gone their own way. Trefyclo actually carries stress on the insignificant penultimate definite article and can justify being written as one word.

The characteristic which most perplexes and even irritates the uninitiated is the seemingly perverse sound change loosely called a mutation. If **tre** (or **tref**) 'town' is to be seen in Trefyclo, why should it become **dre** in Y Drenewydd? If the river name is Cefni, why Llangefni? If the personal name is Mair, then why Llanfair? Rules of mutation are complex but do observe a pattern. They occur in normal speech and therefore in writing. The following is a simplified explanation devised with place-names in mind.

Consonants at the beginning of a word will change in response to a preceding word or consonant in accordance with a set sequence. If we take just the consonant **p** as an example, **pêl** 'ball' could become **y bêl** 'the ball' (soft mutation), **ei phêl** 'her ball' (aspirate mutation), and **fy mhêl** 'my ball' (nasal mutation).

Place-names observe the same patterns. We have Bryn Du 'the black hill' but Afon Ddu 'the black river', because **afon** is a feminine noun and so the adjective takes soft mutation after it. Possession can cause mutation when for example St Dewi's house is Tyddewi, the **caer** associated with Cybi become Caergybi and the **llan** dedicated to Mair become Llanfair. The definite article **y** 'the' (before a consonant) and **yr** (before a vowel or **gw**) results in mutation if the noun following is feminine: **pont** 'bridge' but Y Bont, **gwaun** 'meadow' but Y Waun, **tre newydd** 'new town' but Y Drenewydd.

Finally, note that some adjectives have masculine and feminine forms as in **gwyn** and **gwen** 'white'. Hence Bryn Gwyn but Afon Wen (where **gwen** has undergone a further mutation following a feminine noun).

Here is a summary of the place-names in this book which undergo mutation.

Mutation occurs

in a feminine noun after **y** or **yr**	Allt Melyd, Benllech, Y Bont-faen, Borth-y-gest, Dolgarrog, Y Drenewydd, Y Felinheli, Y Gelli Gandryll, Y Groeslon, Pen-y-bont ar Ogwr, Pen-y-groes, Rossett, Tal-y-bont, Y Waun, Yr Wyddgrug, Ystalyfera
after **yn** or **ym** meaning 'in' and **am** 'near'	Amlwch, Llanfair-ym-Muallt, Llanymddyfri
after the numeral **dau** or **dwy**	Aberdaugleddau, Dwygyfylchi, Penrhyndeudraeth
after the preposition **ar**	Hen-dŷ-gwyn ar Daf, Pontardawe, Pontarddulais
after a feminine noun	Dolgarrog, Dolgellau, Llanbadarn Fawr, Llanfairfechan, Llanilltud Fawr, Moelfre, Rhosllannerchrugog
after a preceding adjective	Dowlais, Hirwaun, Rhuddlan, Rhuthun, Trawsfynydd
to indicate possession	Beddgelert, Caerfyrddin, Caergwrle, Caergybi, Caer-went, Cardiff, Machen, Machynlleth, Rhiwabon, Trearddur, Tredegar, Trefaldwyn,

Trefynwy, Tregaron,
Tyddewi, Ystradgynlais,
all the **llan** names

Selection and presentation of place-names

This volume does not claim to be an exhaustive dictionary of the place-names of Wales. Inevitably, then, selecting the place-names for inclusion has largely been a personal matter, and one for which I must take responsibility. Clearly, the names of major towns and cities have been included and those of the more prominent or well-known villages. However, I am all too conscious of inconsistencies. Occasionally, a place-name may be well-known but the place itself may today appear insignificant on the map. The general rule of thumb I followed, rightly or wrongly, was to include those places which appear in larger type in the Phillip's Great Road Atlas (1991), the scale of which is 1½ miles to 1 inch.

Each entry includes the (Welsh and English) place-name as a head-word. Where one version is merely a spelling variant of the original, the original form (be it Welsh or English) precedes, with the variant in brackets. Where one version is a more substantial phonological variant, no brackets are used. Where there are two names for one place, both well established, the English form precedes in this volume, for the sake of consistency only. This does not in any way imply that the English version has greater authority or antiquity; it is simply a matter of organizational simplicity. There is extensive cross-reference. The sequence of place-names too has been governed by the English rather than the Welsh alphabet. The definite article **Y** or **Yr**, a feature of a number of Welsh place-names, is disregarded for sequencing. After each head-word comes the meaning expressed as a phrase, followed by the elements which make up the place-name. The ensuing paragraph then adds some historical, linguistic, geographical or other commentary. Whenever possible, the first recorded form of the place-name is included (in italics if it is different from the modern form) and also any subsequent forms which may illuminate the development of the name. To avoid confusion, places are located in their pre-1974 counties.

Hills and rivers have been excluded, but inevitably many of them are referred to if they are central to the exposition of place-names. The Index provides a list of all such names which occur in the main text.

In the interests of consistency, I have endeavoured to follow the two authoritative works on the spelling of place-names in Wales namely the *Gazetteer of Welsh Place-names* (1957, 1967) and *Welsh Administrative and Territorial Units* (1969). In cases of doubt, I have consulted the Welsh Office's Place-names Panel.

Abbreviations for the pre-1974 counties of Wales

Anglesey	Angl
Breconshire	Brec
Cardiganshire	Card
Carmarthenshire	Carm
Caernarfonshire	Caern
Denbighshire	Denb
Flintshire	Flints
Glamorgan	Glam
Meirionethshire	Mer
Monmouthshire	Monm
Montgomeryshire	Mont
Pembrokeshire	Pemb
Radnorshire	Radn

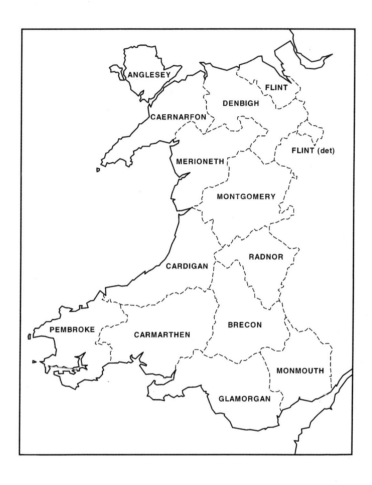

ABERAERON   Card
'mouth of the (river) Aeron'
aber 'river-mouth, estuary'

Aeron means 'goddess of battle', from **aer** 'battle' and a
suffix **-on** which denotes the divine or mythological
association frequently found in river-names. The Latin *ad
ostium Ayron* (1184) refers to the estuary itself as does *aber
aeron* (15th cent.). The town of Aberaeron derives its importance from the harbour which was created in 1807 when the
breakwaters were built.

ABERAFAN   (ABERAVON)   Glam
'mouth of the (river) Afan'
aber 'river-mouth, estuary'

The river (whose route is described in the entry for Cwmafan)
probably takes its name from the personal name Afan or
Afen (*Auan*, *Auen*, *c.* 1150; *Avennae fluvius*, *c.* 1200). The
river-name soon gave its name to the 'vill' of *Aven* (1208) and
to the *Ecclesia de Avene* (*c.* 1291) and eventually the 'vill' was
called Aberafan (*Abber[a]uyn*, *c.* 1400; *Aberavan*, 1548; *Aber
Afan*, 1606). The influence of the Welsh **afon** 'river' and
the English river Avon can be discerned from early on
(*ecclesia de Abbona*, 1348; *Aber Avon*, 1536–9). The 19th-
century docks built at Aberafan Harbour were called Port
Talbot.

ABER-CRAF   Brec
'the stream Craf'
aber 'stream, confluence'

The stream currently called Nant-llech Bellaf passes over the
Henrhyd Falls and enters the river Tawe near Ynys-wen just
east of Aber-craf (*Abercraven*, 1680). It is possible that Craf

was the stream's original name. Craf is **craf** 'garlic', a plant which has medicinal properties and was reputed to ward off the devil. Several streams are called Crafnant.

ABERDÂR   (ABERDARE) Glam
'mouth of the (river) Dâr'
aber 'river-mouth'

The meaning of Dâr is unclear, mainly because the recorded forms are inconsistent (*Aberdar*, 1203; *Aberdaer*, 1348, 1578; *Aberdare*, 1528). A possible origin is **dâr** 'oak' or the element found in **cynddaredd** 'rage'. The town itself is on the confluence of the rivers Dâr and Cynon.

ABERDARON Caern
'mouth of the (river) Daron'
aber 'river-mouth, estuary'

The river Daron rises north of Rhoshirwaun to enter the sea at Aberdaron (1258). Daron was believed to be the goddess of the oak-tree (**dâr** 'oak' as in Aberdare).

ABERDYFI   (ABERDOVEY) Mer
'mouth of the (river) Dyfi'
aber 'river-mouth, estuary'

The earliest documentary evidence (*Aberdewi*, *Aberdiwy*, 12th cent.; *aber dyfi*, 14th cent.) refers to the estuary, while the river-name Dyfi derives from the word **duf** 'dark, black' which became **du** 'black' in modern Welsh. The town emerged in the 19th century along with other resorts and spas in Wales. The form Aberdovey has little to commend it.

ABERGAFENNI (ABERGAVENNY) Y FENNI Monm
'mouth of the (river) Gafenni'
aber 'stream, confluence'

The name of the river can be traced back in records as far as
the 4th century when the Latin documents referred to it as
Gobannio(n). This is a version of an earlier Brythonic word
Gobannia meaning 'river of the blacksmiths' or 'river of the
iron-works' (rather like the modern Welsh word **gof** 'black-
smith'), a reference to the iron-workings which the Romans
exploited. It is known that the Romans built a fort here in
AD 50, so the Brythonic name and iron-workings are probably earlier than that. A later form of the river-name was
Geuenni, c. 1150, while *Abergevenni* and *Abergavenni* also
appear in the 12th century. The river-name came to be used
of the town which stands where the rivers Gafenni and Usk
meet. In Welsh the customary form is Y Fenni; the first
syllable of Gafenni was lost (as in *Bro Venni*, 15th cent., 'the
region of Venni') to be replaced by **y** 'the'.

ABERGELE Denb
'mouth of the (river) Gele'
aber 'river-mouth, estuary'

The name is found as early as the 9th century as *Opergelei*.
Gele is a dialect form of **gelau** 'spear, blade', one of a number
of Welsh river-names describing the action of cutting through
or piercing the land, such as Cleddau 'sword' in Aberdaugleddau or Nodwydd 'needle' found in Anglesey and
Montgomeryshire. It has also been suggested that these rivers
are so-called because their waters flash brightly.

ABERGWAUN see **FISHGUARD**

ABERHONDDU see **BRECON**

ABER-PORTH Card
'estuary in the bay'
aber 'river-mouth, estuary', **porth** 'bay, port, harbour'

There has been very little change in the place-name since the 12th century. The **porth** is the bay into which the river Hoddni or Hoddnant flows (and is actually recorded as *Porth Hodni, c.* 1200; *Blaen Porth Hodnant, c.* 1300). Hoddni (found also in Aberhonddu) contains the word which in modern Welsh is **hawdd** 'easy', but originally meant 'quiet or pleasant'.

ABER-SOCH Caern
'mouth of the (river) Soch'
aber 'river-mouth, estuary'

The river follows a meandering route from the middle of the Llŷn Peninsula, flowing to the west of Carn Fadrun to enter the sea at Aber-soch. Early records refer to it as *Absogh* (1350–1) and *Avon Soch* (1598). Soch is considered to be an Irish word **socc** (as in the river Suck in Connacht) which is related to the Welsh word **hwch** 'sow'. This places the Soch in the category of rivers named after animals that burrow through the land (such as Banw, Ogwen, Aman, Hwch and Twrch). The Irish connection in Llŷn is apparent in a number of place-names including Llŷn or Lleyn itself, which is related to Leinster in Ireland.

ABERSYCHAN Monm
'the stream called Sychan'
aber 'stream, confluence'

The stream Sychan (1616) flows from Blaen Sychan (1659) near Blaenavon (**blaen** 'headwater', **afon** 'river') through Cwm Afon to join with the river Llwyd at Abersychan (*Aber*

4

Sychan, c. 1830). The river-name contains the element **sych** 'dry', probably suggesting a river which dried up in summer because it disappeared underground within its limestone bed.

ABERTAWE see **SWANSEA**

ABERTEIFI see **CARDIGAN**

ABERTYLERI ABERTELERI (ABERTILLERY) Monm 'mouth of the (brook) Teleri'
aber 'stream, confluence'

The brook took its name from a personal name, Teleri, for reasons now lost to us. It is found as Teleri in 1332, but the modern form with **aber** did not appear until much later (*Aber-Tilery*, 1779; *Abertillery*, 1856) probably in association with the industrial town which developed where the brook Teleri joins the river Ebwy Fach. The Welsh forms vary between Abertyleri (the local pronunciation) and Aberteleri.

ABERYSTWYTH   Card
'mouth of the (river) Ystwyth'
aber 'river-mouth, estuary'

The river-name Ystwyth means 'winding' and is found in 1232–3 as *Aberestuuth*, and in the 14th century as *aber ystwyth*. The original Norman castle was built, as the name suggests, on the Ystwyth in 1110. However, in 1211 another castle was built near the estuary of the river Rheidol a mile and a half to the north, taking the name with it; this became the site of the modern town.

ALLT MELYD see **MELIDEN**

AMLWCH   Angl
'near the pool'
am 'near, beside, around', **llwch** 'pool', 'mud, swamp' or
'inlet'

The name is recorded from the 13th century onwards (such as
Amelogh, 1352; *Amloch*, 1547). The second element **llwch**
with this meaning is not found in the everyday usage of
modern Welsh. It probably refers to the area, formerly
swampy, near the present church. However, **llwch** may well
have meant 'inlet', referring to the creek which later became
the harbour of Porth Amlwch.

AMMANFORD   RHYDAMAN   Carm
'ford on the (river) Aman'
rhyd 'ford'

The river-name *Aman* (which appeared in 1541 as *Amman*)
came from an older *Amanw* which itself derives from the
word *banw* 'pig' or 'piglet', suggesting a river which rooted its
way through the ground. The site was occupied simply by a
tavern, the Cross Inn, until the late 19th century when the
town gradually developed around the tavern and was called
Ammanford, subsequently translated as Rhydaman.

BAE COLWYN see **COLWYN BAY**

BAGLAN   Glam

The now disused church at Baglan (*Bagelan*, 1199) (which
stands in the churchyard of the modern St Catherine's
church) was dedicated to St Baglan, but 'Llanfaglan' (as
found in Llanfaglan in Caernarfonshire) either did not
survive or, as is more likely, was never used. There are other
places in Wales which simply preserve a saint's name, such as
Ceidio and Gwytherin.

BALA   Mer
'outlet'
bala 'outlet'; 'narrow land between two lakes'

Bala is one of a group of common nouns which became
place-names, hence the consistent use of the definite article
(*la Bala*, 1331; *y bala*, 14th century; *the Bala*, 1582; *o vala
Lhyn Tegid, c.* 1700), which is why the town is referred to as
Y Bala. The river Dee flows from Llyn Tegid (*Thlintegit*,
1285) at Bala.

BANGOR   Caern
'a wattled fence'
bangor 'the plaited cross-bar strengthening the top of a
wattled fence'

The ecclesiastical settlement or monastic site at Bangor
(*Benchoer*, 634) was protected by a wattled fence strength-
ened by a distinctive plaited top called a *bangor*. There is a
Bangor in Ulster and another in Flintshire, both ecclesiastical
sites, and it was commonly believed that both derived from
the Caernarfonshire Bangor. However, there are in Wales
other examples of Bangor which were not churches; the name
also occurs in Brittany. The likely conclusion is that *bangor*
became a common word for a site, ecclesiastical or secular,
which was protected by such a plaited fence.

BARGOED   BARGOD   Glam
'boundary'
bargod 'border, boundary, edge; eaves'

The river Bargod flows from Mynydd y Fochriw into the
Rhymni at Aberbargoed (*Aber Bargoed*, 1578). It was
customary to refer to the river as Bargod Rhymni (*Bargau*

Remni, c. 1170) to distinguish it from Bargod Taf (*Berkehu Taf, c.* 1170) which also rises on Mynydd y Fochriw and flows down Cwm Bargod and into the Taf near Treharris. Rivers have habitually been regarded as boundaries and Bargod Rhymni seems to have marked off the land at Brithdir from other land in the commote of Senghennydd uwch Caeach. With the industrial and urban development of the 18th and 19th centuries Aberbargoed was retained as a name for the settlement on the eastern side of the river, and the railway junction and station on the west at the new Bargoed Junction became the town of Bargoed. The change from Bargod to Bargoed (seen from the 16th century onwards) is probably a reflection of over-zealous restoration of what was incorrectly perceived as the element **coed** 'trees', since **-oe-** is frequently pronounced **-o-** colloquially. The change may have been reinforced by the existence nearby of Penycoed, Argoed, Oakdale and Blackwood.

BARMOUTH   Y BERMO   Mer
'mouth of the (river) Mawddach'
aber 'estuary'

Originally, the river-name was Mawdd and the estuary 'Aber-Mawdd', which in turn became Abermaw (*Abermau*, 1284) and in modern Welsh Abermo and Y Bermo (where the first syllable of Abermo is taken to be the definite article **y**). The English version of 'Aber-Mawdd' was something like 'Abermouth' (*Abermowth*, 1410) which became Barmouth, possibly influenced by the 'mouth' of the river. Today the river is called Mawddach, but originally that was the name of a tributary of the Mawdd (with **-ach** being a dimunutive ending, 'the little Mawdd'). Mawdd is also to be seen in the name of the area Mawddwy 'the territory of Mawdd'.

Y BARRI   (BARRY)   Glam
'hill brook'
barr 'summit of a hill'

The hill at Barry town was the **barr**; the stream there was called *Barren* (13th cent.). In time, *Barren* came to be used of the settlement itself and of the island. The linguistic development was from *Barren* to *Barre* (*Isle of Barre*, 1510) and then to Barri anglicized as Barry (*Barry Island*, 1610). The channel between the island and mainland was called Aberbarri (*Aberbarrey*, 1536–9). Today, the town is referred to as Y Barri or Barry and the island is Ynys y Barri or Barry Island.

BEAUFORT   (Y) CENDL   Monm

In 1780, the duke of Beaufort granted a lease of the site to four members of the Kendall family from the north of England, one of whom, Edward Kendall, built the ironworks. For some time, the name of the works and associated village was Cendl (a Welsh spelling of Kendall) and, in literary texts, Y Cendl, until it was replaced (at least in English usage) by Beaufort.

BEAUMARIS   BIWMARES   Angl
'fair marsh'
Norman-French **beau**, **marais**

The castle and town of Beaumaris were built on the open former marshland beside the Menai Strait. Latin documents refer to it as *Bello Marisco* (1284) and when the borough received its charter in 1296 it was as *Beaumaris*. The Welsh pronunciation has always been very close to *Bewemarras* as recorded in 1489 and *Bewmares* in 1612.

BEDDGELERT   Caern
'the grave of Celert'
bedd 'grave'

The village's name is first recorded in the 13th century
(*Bekelert*, 1258; *Bedkelert*, 1281). The identity of Celert is not
known, but he was certainly a man and not a dog. From at
least the 16th century, the village came to be associated with
the legend of Gelert, the faithful hound of Prince Llywelyn
(in a Welsh version of an international folk-tale). In the 18th
century the tradition was further popularized when a
commemorative stone was erected on the supposed site of the
dog's grave.

BEDWAS   Monm
'grove of birch trees'
bedwos 'grove of small birch trees' (from **bedw** 'birch')

The word **bedwos** was associated with a profusion of under-
growth and young hazel and birch trees, usually on a slope.
Variation of **-os**, **-as**, and **-es** are common; this parish was
Bedewas (*c.* 1102) and *Bedwes, a birche grove* (in 1536–9). In
parts of mid and north-east Wales the word became **betwos** 'a
wooded slope' and later **betws** (not to be confused with the
entirely different **betws** 'bead-house' which appears in place-
names like Betws-y-coed).

BENLLECH   Angl
'(the) capstone'
pen 'head, top', **llech** 'stone'

The flat capstone of a cromlech was **y benllech** 'the top stone';
cromlech 'the circular stone' contains the same element. This
particular cromlech had a distinctively large capstone, from
which a nearby farm took its name as Tyddyn y Benllech

10

'cottage of the capstone' (**y** 'the'). It was Tyddyn y Benllech which gave the 18th-century village the name Y Benllech or simply Benllech.

Y BERMO see BARMOUTH

BETHESDA   Caern

The Welsh Nonconformist chapel was built in 1820 and given the biblical name Bethesda. In common with many villages which grew up around chapels the village took the name of the chapel.

BETWS-Y-COED   Caern
'prayer-house in the wood'
betws 'prayer house', **y** 'the', **coed** 'wood'

Betws, common in Wales, and perceived to be a Welsh word, is in fact derived from the Old English word **bed-hūs**, 'an oratory, a house or cell dedicated to prayer', where **bed** means 'prayer' (and consequently 'bead' as in 'rosary bead') and **hūs** is 'house'. The first record of it is as *Betus* in 1254 and, although there is one reference to it as *o vetws y koed* in 1352, the present name seems not to have come into general use until the 18th century. At one time it was also known as Betws Wyrion Iddon 'the descendants or family of Iddon'.

BIWMARES see BEAUMARIS

BLACKWOOD   COED-DUON   Monm
'the black wood', 'the black trees'
coed 'trees', **duon** plural of **du** 'black'

Early references are to *Coed-dduon* (1833) and *Blackwood* (1856).

11

BLAENAFON (BLAENAVON)   Monm
'headwater of the river'
blaen 'headwater', **afon** 'river'

The river Sychan flows from Blaen Sychan near Blaenavon (*Blaen Avon*, 1532–3). (See also the entry for Abersychan.)

BLAENAU (BLAINA)   Monm
'uplands'
blaenau (plural of **blaen**) 'heights, uplands, headwaters'

Commonly referred to as Blaenau Gwent (as in *Blaine Gwent*, 1594), where Gwent (broadly corresponding to modern Monmouthshire and formerly the name of a Welsh kingdom) meant 'field' and later 'market-place'. The industrial Blaenau developed in the 19th century out of the parish of *Aberystruth* ('mouth of the stream *Ystrwyth*' and not to be confused with Aberystwyth), as in *Aberystrwyth Blaeney Gwent* (1590).

BLAENAU FFESTINIOG   / Mer
'the uplands of Ffestiniog'
blaenau (plural of **blaen**) 'heights, uplands, headwaters'

Ffestiniog is recorded in 1419 as *Festynyok* and means 'the territory of Ffestin' (or possibly **ffestiniog** 'a defensive position'). Blaenau Ffestiniog itself is a 19th-century industrial development some two miles to the north of Ffestiniog, and the centre of considerable slate-quarrying.

BLAENAVON see **BLAENAFON**

BLAINA see **BLAENAU**

Y BONT-FAEN see **COWBRIDGE**

BORTH-Y-GEST . Caern

'harbour of the paunch'
porth 'harbour, cove', **y** 'the', **cest** 'paunch', 'hollow'

The dominant feature of the landscape north of the harbour and the Glaslyn estuary is the hill called *Gest* (1306–7), modern Moel y Gest (**moel** 'bare hill'), whose shape prompted the comparison with a paunch or big belly and which gave its name to a fairly extensive medieval township called Gest. However, it has been argued that the belly could allude figuratively to a vast bog which swallows everything. There was such a Cest near Tremadog; Moel y Gest overlooks this bog and may have taken its name, with Borth-y-gest in turn taking its name from Moel y Gest. A modification of this is that **cest** may refer to the undulating belly-like hills and hollows of low-lying moorland, as in Rhos-y-bol (**rhos** 'moorland', **bol** 'belly') in Anglesey. Whatever the precise significance of **cest**, the place-name is Borth-y-gest rather than 'Porth-y-gest' probably because it was customary to refer to it as 'Y Borth' or simply 'Borth', but the emergence of Porthmadog in the mid-19th century necessitated the addition of a distinguishing identification (although Porthmadog may actually have reduced Borth-y-gest's importance as a harbour at the entrance to the estuary). The harbour was referred to at one time as *Gest harbour* (1748).

BRECON   ABERHONDDU Brec

'land of Brychan'   'mouth of the (river) Honddu'
aber 'stream, confluence'

The original name was Brycheiniog (as in *Brecheniauc*, 1100); where Brychan is the name of a 5th-century prince and **-iog** 'land of'. Anglicization caused Brycheiniog to become the now antiquarian and archaic Brecknok or Brecknock (frequently used as the county name), and Brychan to become

Brecon. The Welsh name for the town, Aberhonddu (*Aberhotheni*, 1191), includes **aber** 'confluence, mouth of a stream' and the river-name Hoddni, modern Honddu, which joins the river Usk at Brecon.

BRIDGEND PEN-Y-BONT AR OGWR Glam
'end of the bridge' 'end of the bridge over (the river) Ogwr'
pen 'end', **y** 'the', **pont** 'bridge', **ar** 'on'

The bridge itself is believed to date from 1425 (*Bryggen Eynde*, 1444). It is likely that both English and Welsh forms (*Pennebont*, 1536–9) have always been used. A Norman castle is said to have been located here to control the river crossing. The original name of the river is seen in *Ocmur* (*c.* 1150) and *Ogemor* (1314). In English speech it became Ogmore, the name of the river, the Vale of Ogmore, the Forest of Ogmore and Ogmore-by-sea. In Welsh speech *Ocmur* became *Ogfur* and then Ogwr. Ogmore and Ogwr comprise **og** 'sharp' or 'rapid' (an element occurring in several river-names, such as Ogwen or Ogwan in Nant Ffrancon) and an unknown -**mur**.

BRITON FERRY LLANSAWEL (2) Glam
'the ferry at the farm near the bridge', 'church of (St) Sawel'
Old English **brycg** 'bridge', Old English **tūn** 'farm', **ferry** 'ferry', Welsh **llan** 'church'

Nothing is known of a bridge except as part of the place-name Briton (*Brigeton,* 1201; *Brytton*, 1315; *Briton*, 1447), but there was a ferry here across the river Neath (*Britan Ferry caullid in Walsche Llanisauel*, 1536–9). The spelling Britton Ferry has been commonly used. The church dedication was to the same Sawel (or Sawyl) as in Llansawel in Carmarthenshire.

BROUGHTON

Flints

'the farm by the brook'
Old English **brōc** 'brook', Old English **tūn** 'farm'

The place appears in the Domesday Book of 1086 as *Brochetune*. The brook itself is called the Broughton Brook. Fairly recently a Welsh form of the name, Brychdyn, has emerged (especially in the media). Linguistically, this is perfectly acceptable and is in keeping with other Welsh forms of English place-names in Flintshire (such as Sychdyn, Golftyn, Mostyn and Prestatyn). There is another Broughton near Wrexham which does have an accredited Welsh form Brychdyn (*Brochtyn*, *c.* 1700). However, in the more anglicized area between Queensferry, Hawarden and Chester there is no historical evidence of this Broughton ever being called Brychdyn.

BRYMBO

Denb

'hill of dirt'
bryn 'hill', **baw** 'dirt'

Brymbo has been associated with the steel, iron and coal industries, and early references (*Brynbawe*, 1391; *Brinbawe*, 1412) could suggest a spoil heap produced by medieval mining. However, since the same or a similar name occurs elsewhere where there is no evidence of industrial excavation (as in Brymbo near Eglwys-bach, Denbighshire and Cwm Baw near Llanllugan, Montgomeryshire), **baw** may simply have described dirty, muddy conditions underfoot, possibly associated with steep hills. The change from **-n-** to **-m-** (*Brymbo*, 1480) is influenced by the following **-b-** (as in Llanbedr Pont Steffan becoming Llambed and Lampeter); the change from **-aw** to **-o** is usual especially at the unaccented end of a word (as in Abermaw becoming Y Bermo).

BRYNAMAN   Carm
'hill of the (river) Aman'
bryn 'hill'

The two tributaries Aman Fawr and Aman Fach (**mawr** 'big',
bach 'small') rise on the southern slopes of the Black
Mountain and join north of Rhosaman (**rhos** 'moor') to flow
past Brynaman and through Cwm Aman on to Glanaman to
join the river Loughor south of Ammanford. (See the entry
for Ammanford for the significance of the river-name.) The
bryn here is one of the lower hills of the Black Mountain. The
earlier name was Gwter Fawr 'great channel, gutter' (*Guter
vaur*, 1805), with Brynaman emerging a little later (*Bryn
Amman*, 1844); both names were in use for some time
(*Brynaman neu'r Gwtter Fawr* 1875, **neu'r** 'or the').

BRYNBUGA see **USK**

BRYN-MAWR   Brec
'big hill'
bryn 'hill', **mawr** 'big'

The growth of Bryn-mawr can be ascribed to industrial
development in the 19th century. Until 1832 the site was
called Gwaun-helygen (**gwaun** 'moorland', **helygen** 'willow-
tree'); this was replaced (in all probability, deliberately) by
the simpler, more memorable name of another part of the
same area.

BUCKLEY   BWCLE   Flints
'the wood of the bucks'
Old English **bucc** 'buck', Old English **lēah** 'wood, clearing in a
wood'

A deer park was created here by Roger de Mohault (Mold)
some time after 1241 but was destroyed by Llywelyn ap

Gruffudd in 1257. The early forms of the place-name show a number of forms in -o- (such as *Bokkeley*, 1294) as well as in -u- (such as *Bukkelee*, 1301–2) leading to the belief that Buckley contains the word **bōc** 'beech', a reference to the many beech-trees in the area. However, the beech was not seen in north Wales until the 18th century when it was extensively planted in large estates. The variation in -o- and -u- was reinforced by Welsh usage which still preserves the early English pronunciation (seen for example in *Boucle*, 1326).

BUILTH (WELLS)   LLANFAIR-YM-MUALLT   Brec
'cow-pasture' 'church of (St) Mary in Buallt'
bu 'cow', **gellt** (modern **gwellt**) 'pasture', **llan** 'church'

The original name was Buellt (from **bu** and **gellt**) and is recorded as *Buelt* in the 10th century. Builth is an anglicized spelling and pronunciation of this form. In the 19th century the local chalybeate springs gave the opportunity to promote the town as a spa and caused the addition of Wells to the original name. The parish was Llanfair-ym-Muallt, 'the church of St Mary in Buallt'. The change from Buellt to Buallt was probably the result of a presumed reference to **allt** 'hill'.

BURRY PORT   Carm
'the port of the sand-dune'
bury 'a burrow'

Several place-names in the region include the word Burry. One is the well-attested river in the Gower peninsula, just across the Loughor estuary, the river Burry (*Borry*, 1318; *Burry*, 1323; *Byrri*, 14th cent.); another is the island Burry Holms. This name is a late (19th cent.) name for the port on the edge of the Pembre Burrows. The word **burrows** for sand-

17

dunes occurs frequently on the south Wales coast and is presumably associated with rabbit warrens; **bury** and **burry** occur as variants of the singular **burrow**. This explanation is preferable to the suggestion that **bury** signifies 'fort' (as found at the end of many place-names in England).

BWCLE see **BUCKLEY**

CAERDYDD see **CARDIFF**

CAERFFILI (CAERPHILLY)   Glam
'the fort of Ffili'
caer 'fort'

Ffili's identity is unknown. In 1268 the fort was the centre of the cantref of Senghennydd and then a Norman castle (*Kaerfili*, 1271). The anglicized spelling has been in use for many centuries (as in *Kaerphilly*, 1314).

CAERGWRLE   Flints
'the fort of the crane-wood'
caer 'fort', Old English **cron**, **corn** 'crane', Old English **lēah** 'wood' or 'clearing in a wood'

This deceptively Welsh name is for the large part English. The town and castle played a part in establishing administrative and military control by the Mercians who named the town 'Corley', to which the Welsh prefixed **caer** in reference to the castle (*Caergorlei*, 1327). The English name referred to the crane, the bird which must have frequented the **lēah**, the wood or clearing in the wood; the same name is to be found in Corley in Warwickshire. In common with many other English place-names in north-east Wales, the place-name became naturalized and followed the usages of Welsh pronunciation and spelling. The resulting name prompted various imaginative and creative attempts at providing an appropriate explanation. One notable example was that of the mythological giant Gwrle, who was reputed to have lived in the castle and to have been buried a short distance away at Cefn-y-bedd in a neolithic burial mound.

CAERGYBI see HOLYHEAD

CAERLEON   CAERLLION-AR-WYSG   Monm
'fort of the legions' 'Caerllion on the river Wysg (Usk)'
Welsh **caer** 'fort', Latin **legionum** 'of the legions', Welsh **ar** 'on'

The Second Legion had its base here at what the Romans called Isca Legionis ('Isca of the legion'). The Welsh word **caer** was used of the Roman fort so that *c.* 800 the fort was referred to as *Cair Legeion guar Usic* (Uisc), and *c.* 1150 as *Cairlion, civitas legionum* ('the city of the legions'). The original British river-name became the Roman Isca, and the modern Wysg and Usk.

CAERNARFON   Caern
'the fort in Arfon'
caer 'fort', **yn** 'in'

Caernarfon is 'Caer yn Arfon' (as in *Kaer yn Arvon*, 1258). Arfon itself was a cantref extending from Bangor to Yr Eifl, and took its name from its location 'ar Fôn', 'opposite or facing Môn' (Anglesey). Caernarfon was also a Roman stronghold and was called Segontium by them; a name based on the British river-name (which was something like Segont which contains the element **sego** 'strong, powerful'). The river-name became *Seynt* (1284) and eventually Saint. The variant Seiont (*Seiont flu.*, 1570) is an antiquarian restoration.

CAERPHILLY see CAERFFILI

CAERSŴS   Mont
'the fort of Swys'
caer 'fort'

This was possibly the site of a Romano-British fort (hence
caer) but the association with a later Swys is difficult to
explain. Tradition has it that Swys was a queen, Swys Wen,
and that the fort was Caer Swys Wen. Caersŵs did not exist
as a borough much before the 14th or even the 15th century.
Other forms are *Caerswys* (14th cent.) and *Caer-soos, Caer-
swŝs* (*c.* 1700). The form Caersws (without the circumflex) is
more generally used today.

CAER-WENT   Monm
'the fort of Gwent'
caer 'fort'

The Roman fort and town of Venta Silurum was based on
the town occupied by the south-east Wales tribe called the
Silures. The town came to be referred to simply as Venta
(which meant 'field' and then 'market'), which in time
became Gwent. (The Venta of the Roman Venta Belgarum
became the **Win-** in Winchester, with -**chester** corresponding
to the **caer** in Caer-went *Kaerwent*, 1254.) The Normans
established a new base to the east on the river Wye which
came to be called Cas-gwent or Chepstow. (See the entry for
Chepstow for further information.)

CALDICOT   Monm
'cold hut'
Old English **cald** 'cold, inhospitable', Old English **cot** 'hut,
refuge'

A number of place-names contain the element **cot**, which
usually indicates a hut some distance away from a farm or

village which could be used as a store or as a refuge in bad weather. In England the place-name takes the form Caldecote, Caldecott or Calcott and forms recorded for this Caldicot are very similar (*Caldecote*, 1086; *Caldicote*, 1286; *Calecote*, 1381). Related to **cot** are **cottage** and the Welsh word **cwt** 'hut'. In this instance the **cot** was presumably cold because it was exposed to the winds of the Severn Estuary.

CAPEL CURIG   Caern
'the chapel of (St) Curig'
capel 'chapel'

The Welsh **capel** and English **chapel** are derived independently from Latin **capella** (with **chapel** coming via French). It can mean a 'house of prayer' but usually it signifies a small church distant from the parish church, perhaps erected within a private estate, or occasionally as a smaller church for parishioners in a remote area. Early forms are *Capel Kiryg* (1536–9) and *Capel Kerig* (1578, influenced by **cerrig** 'stones', a pronunciation which is still heard locally).

CARDIFF   CAERDYDD   Glam
'fort on the (river) Taf'
caer 'fort'

The genitive singular of Taf was Tyf a form which possibly goes back to the 6th century. Hence 'Caer-Dyf' 'the fort of the Taf' (as in *Kairdif*, 1106). It was 'Caerdyf' which produced the anglicized form Cardiff, in much the same way that the river-name Taf was anglicized to Taff, and later the cathedral Llandaf became Llandaff (with the additional modification of the stress moving to the first syllable as happened in Cardiff). The Welsh pronunciation of 'Caerdyf' as Caerdydd (as in *o gaer dydd*, 1566; and *Caer Didd*, 1698)

shows the colloquial alternation of Welsh **-f** and **-dd**. Taf is
related to a group of Celtic river-names (such as Thames,
Tame, Tamar and Tawe in Abertawe) meaning 'water' (or
possibly 'dark').

CARDIGAN   ABERTEIFI   Card
'land of Ceredig' 'mouth of the (river) Teifi'
aber 'river-mouth'

Cardigan (*Kerdigan*, 1194) is the anglicized form of Ceredigion
(*cereticiaun*, 12th cent.) which is the 5th-century personal name
Ceredig with the territorial suffix **-ion** 'land of Ceredig'.
(Ceredig was popularly believed to be one of the sons of
Cunedda, the legendary 5th-century leader from the north of
Britain who established the dynasty of Gwynedd.) This 'land
of Ceredig' encompassed land to the east of the modern town,
but from the 13th century Ceredigion and Cardiganshire came
to be the name of the much more extensive medieval shire. The
anglicized Cardigan, however, was restricted to the town, an
unusual development which reverses the usual pattern of shires
taking names of country towns. In Welsh the town is Aberteifi
(*Aberteivi*, 1191) from its location on the estuary of the river
Teifi. Although the river-name is recorded from the 2nd
century the meaning is obscure.

CARMARTHEN   CAERFYRDDIN   Carm
'fort at Maridunum'
caer 'fort'

Maridunum 'the fort near the sea' was the name of the
Roman camp here, a version of a British place-name
comprising the elements which today give us **môr** 'sea' and
din 'fort'. Maridunum developed into Myrddin by which time
the **din** element was not recognized as the word meaning
'fort'; hence the addition of the tautologous **caer** 'fort'. In

addition, Myrddin was wrongly perceived as a personal name, in particular that of a legendary 6th-century warrior whom Geoffrey of Monmouth incorporated into the Arthurian legend (after latinizing Myrddin to Merlinus).

CARMEL   Caern
The village adopted the name of the Nonconformist chapel which commemorated the biblical mountain of Carmel which is appropriate to the location.

CAS-GWENT see **CHEPSTOW**

CASLLWCHWR see **LOUGHOR**

CEDWELI see **CYDWELI**

CEFN-MAWR   Denb
'big ridge'
cefn 'ridge', **mawr** 'large'

Cefn-mawr is on high ground between the river Dee and Rhosymedre.

CEMAES   Angl
'inlets' or 'bends'
cemais plural of **camas** 'bend in a river or coastline, a bay'

The 'inlets' possibly refer to the bay and adjacent coastline at Cemaes (*Kemmeys*, 1291–2; *Kemmes alias Kemmays*, 1461). The old name was Porth Wygyr (*portu yoiger in Monia*, 1194; *porth wygyr* 15th cent.), the harbour of the river Wygyr (*Gwegyr*, 1451); Gwygyr is possibly a personal name. The **cemais** may well have been the bends in the river just before it reaches the beach. The preferred spelling Cemais has been supplanted in general usage by a spelling which supposes the name to contain **maes** 'field'.

CENDL see **BEAUFORT**

CERRIGYDRUDION   Denb
'stones of the heroes'
cerrig plural of **carreg** 'stone', **y** 'the', **drudion** plural of **drud**
'hero, fighter'

This was a common enough name (six in Anglesey, two in
Caernarfonshire for example), adopted usually by a croft or
cottage, and probably an allusion to heroic building feats or
to the fortitude of the inhabitants. Here the name became
that of a village (*Kericdrudion*, 1254), but by the 16th century
there is clear evidence that people perceived the name to be
modelled on the English word **druid** (*Kerrig Druidion*, *c.*
1700), an association reinforced by the stones of druidic
circles and later by the eisteddfodic *gorsedd*.

CHEPSTOW   CAS-GWENT   Monm
'market-place' 'castle in Gwent'
Old English **cēap** 'market', **stow** 'place', Welsh **cas (castell)**
'castle'

The modern Cas-gwent (*Cas-gwent*, 1612) is an abbreviation
of an earlier 'Castell-gwent' (*castell guent*, 1150), as happened
with Casnewydd, Monmouthshire. Interestingly the name
Gwent itself, the Venta Silurum of the Romans, seems to have
meant 'field' and then taken on the connotation of 'market'; it
was possibly this strategic location which gave rise to
Chepstowe (1308) and *Chapestowe* (1338) 'the market-place'.

CHIRK   Y WAUN   Denb
'(the river) Ceiriog' 'the moorland'
y 'the', **gwaun** 'moorland'

Chirk (*Chirk*, 1295; *Cheyrk*, 1309) is an anglicized form of the

24

river Ceiriog, which flows from the Berwyn mountains through Glyn Ceiriog and Chirk. (Ceiriog was probably a personal name originally.) Chirk was the centre of the Norman lordship of Chirkland, and it is this influence which probably explains the anglicization. The Welsh name of the lordship, Swydd y Waun, and of the town, Y Waun (*Ewevn*, 1291; *Y Waun*, 1368), refer to the moorland near Chirk Castle.

CILGETI   (KILGETTY)   Pemb
'the nook of Ceti'
cil 'nook, corner'

Nothing is known of Ceti. The name is also associated with Ynys Geti (Sketty) in Glamorgan. The earliest recorded form is *Kylketty* (1330).

CINMEL   (KINMEL)   Denb
'the nook of Mael'
cil 'corner, nook, shelter'

The exact significance of the shelter is lost to us, although earlier forms (such as *Kilmeyl*, 1331) testify to its existence. The identity of Mael is also obscure, leading some to argue that it is **mael** 'prince'. The change from **-l-** to **-n-** (*Kynmayll*, 1515–16) is probably caused by the following **-m-.**

CLYDACH   Glam

There are a number of rivers called Clydach, all in south Wales, with eight in Glamorgan alone. Two of them are only a short distance from each other. The Upper Clydach (*Higher Clydach*, *c.* 1700) flows from Gwaun Caegurwen into the river Tawe at Pontardawe. The Lower Clydach (*c.* 1700) flows from Mynydd y Betws (or Mynydd y Gwair) through Cwm Clydach (**cwm** 'narrow valley') and into the river Tawe at Aberclydach (*c.* 1700) (**aber** 'river-mouth'), now the town called Clydach. The earliest forms recorded for some of the Clydach rivers (such as *Cloeda*, 1129; *Cleudach*, 1147; *Cloudach, c.* 1150) point to an Irish word. Claudagh, Claddagh and Cloydagh, for example, occur in Ireland as river-names and village-names, meaning sometimes a rocky beach, sometimes a wild rocky river. The latter appears to be the meaning in Wales. It is further argued that the Irish influence explains the form Clydach, since the usual Welsh river-name would have been Clywedog (found in mid and north Wales), although it has been customary to explain Clywedog as deriving from **clywed** 'listen', giving the sense of a 'noisy river'. The dialectal pronunciation (as 'Clidach', 'Cleidach' or 'Cloidach') seems to confirm the derivation. The river-name Clydach may therefore be a distant relative of the Scottish Clyde.

CLYNNOG Caern
'abounding in holly'
celyn 'holly', **-awg, -og** (adjectival ending)

The older forms *Kelynnauk* (*c.* 1291) and *Kellynnawc* (1346) indicate an area where holly grew in profusion. The adjectival **-og** appears quite frequently to indicate an abundance as in Eithinog (**eithin** 'gorse') and Cegidog (**cegid** 'hemlock'). Clynnog was also known as Clynnog Fawr (*Kelynnauk Vaur, c.* 1291, **mawr** 'great') as it was the principal church established by and dedicated to Beuno, the 5th-century saint. Clynnog Fechan (**fechan** 'small') was at Llangeinwen in Anglesey, so-called because Clynnog Fawr owned the parish land at Llangeinwen.

COED-DUON see **BLACKWOOD**

COED-POETH   Denb
'burnt trees'
coed 'trees', **poeth** 'burnt, hot'

There was considerable industrial exploitation of the surrounding area (in Minera, Bersham and Brymbo). However,
the early occurrence of Coed-poeth (*Coid poch*, 1391; *Coed
Poeth*, 1412; *Rhôs y coed poeth, c.* 1700) suggests that the area
was cleared by burning, possibly in order to facilitate mining,
well before the major industrial developments.

COLWYN BAY   BAE COLWYN   Denb
'bay of the (river) Colwyn'
bae 'bay'

A number of rivers or brooks are named after animals (such
as Twrch 'boar' near Llanuwchlyn and Ystalyfera, and Hwch
'sow' near Llanberis). There are several brooks named after
colwyn 'a young animal', 'a whelp', 'a pet dog'. The river
Colwyn (*Avon Colloine*, 1638; *Avon Golwyn alias Avon
Benmen*, 1684–5) flows from near Llanelian yn Rhos into the
sea to the west of Penmaen Rhos, through the original township of Colwyn (*Coloyne*, 1334). In the 19th century the
Victorian interest in seaside resorts encouraged expansion
westwards to create the modern town of Colwyn Bay,
emulated by the Welsh Bae Colwyn. It was this development
which necessitated the addition of the distinguishing
appellatives Hen and Old for the original township.

CONNAH'S QUAY   Flints

The gradual silting of the river Dee meant that a new channel
(called the New Cut) had to be opened in 1737. A new system
of docks became a prerequisite for industrial expansion and
in particular for facilitating the export of coal. One such quay

was the *New Quay* (1832) and another was *Connas Quay* (1791), the former name being used of the pier itself, the latter of the area around the pier. In time, only the name Connah's Quay survived. The precise identity of Connah is uncertain. Some believe him to have been the local inn-keeper. However, the family was certainly prominent in the industry and commerce of the area.

CONWY   Caern
'(place on) the (river) Conwy'

The Romans had a fort called Canovium at Caerhun, four miles south of the present town and close to the river Conwy. Canovium is a latinized form of the British river-name which became Conwy, the modern name of the river (*Coneway*, 1290). The town of Conwy developed on the estuary (**aber**) of the river Conwy and was originally called Aberconwy (*Aberconuy*, 12th cent.). During the last three hundred years the town has been referred to as Conwy or the anglicized Conway (*Conway als Aberconway*, 1698). More recently, Aberconwy has been restored as the name of an administrative district, and the anglicized spelling Conway is no longer used in official communication.

CORWEN   Mer
'sanctuary stone'
côr 'sanctuary, channel', or **cor** 'small', **maen** 'stone'

The church in Corwen has a reputedly ancient stone called Carreg-y-Big, 'the pointed stone', built into the porch. This stone may well have been a standing stone, a **maen-hir** 'long-stone, monolith, menhir'. The **côr** may therefore have referred to the church or to pagan ritual popularly associated with the **maen-hir**, so that 'sacred stone' would be a more appropriate meaning. However, it has been argued that the

28

first element is **cor** 'small'. The earliest forms (*Corvaen*, 1254; *Korvaen*, 14th cent.) can be interpreted either way. Corwen is a natural enough development (with **-f-** changing to **-w-**) and begins to appear in the 15th century (*Corwen*, 1443), probably influenced by the word **wen** 'white' which is the mutated form of **gwen** 'white'.

COWBRIDGE   Y BONT-FAEN   Glam
'bridge used by cows' 'the stone bridge'
y 'the', **pont** 'bridge', **maen** 'stone'

The first bridge may well have been habitually used by, or specifically built for, cattle being driven to the market, but whatever the reason the name is very well established (*Coubrugge*, 1263). Cowbridge is on the site of a Roman settlement (where the Roman road between Cardiff and Neath crosses the river Thaw), and the name of the settlement, intriguingly, was Bovium which scholars derive from a British word for 'cow' (rather than from the Latin word). However, this may be a coincidence. Another bridge (**pont**) of stone (**maen**) nearby gave the town its Welsh name Y Bont-faen (*Bontvaen, c.* 1500).

CRICIETH   Caern
'mound of the captives'
crug 'hill, mound', **caith** (plural of **caeth**) 'captives'

The Norman castle (*Crukeith*, 1273) was located strategically on the hill (**crug**) above the sea and it was certainly used as a prison. The modern pronunciation as Cricieth began to emerge in the 15th century The occasional spelling with **-cc-** (as Criccieth) is an attempt to demonstrate the **-gc-** in the historical etymology of *crug-caith*; however, such a form has no basis in standard Welsh spelling.

CRUCYWEL (CRICKHOWELL)   Brec
'Hywel's mound'
crug 'cairn, mound'

Although **crug** does mean 'hill' it is also associated with a man-made mound or cairn of stones. Consequently, **crug** is frequently found in relation to a prehistoric site on a hill. (For another example, see the entry for Yr Wyddgrug.) In this instance the mound is reputedly the Iron Age fort to the north of Crickhowell locally referred to as Crug Hywel or Table Mountain (*Crichoel*, 1263; *Crukhowell*, 1281). The identity of Hywel is not known, but the anglicized spelling as Crick- is also to be seen in Crick (Monmouthshire), Crickadarn (Crucadarn, Breconshire) and Crickheath (Shropshire).

CRYMYCH   Pemb
'crooked stream'
crwm 'bent'

The stream took its name (*Crymmych*, 1584; *Nant Crymich*, 1652) from its meandering course as a minor tributary of the river Nevern. However, the village appears to have taken its name more directly from the tavern called the Crymych Arms established at the roadside.

CWMAFAN   Glam
'valley of the (river) Afan'
cwm 'valley, combe'

The river Afan (which is discussed in the entry for Aberafan) rises on Mynydd Blaenafan and flows through the valley of Cwm Afan and the town of Cwmafan to enter the sea at Aberafan.

CWM-BRÂN   Monm
'the valley of the (river) Brân'
cwm 'valley'

The valley is referred to in 1707 as *Cwmbran*, but the town did not come into being until 1949 when it was developed as a 'new town'. The designated location was at the junction of Nant Brân (**nant** 'brook') and the river Llwyd (**afon** 'river', **llwyd** 'grey'). The meaning of **brân** is 'raven' and, as a river-name, it probably refers to dark waters rather than to a brook frequented by the raven. However, Brân is also a personal name.

CYDWELI (CEDWELI) (KIDWELLY)   Carm
'land of Cadwal'

The place-name is first recorded in the 10th century as *Cetgueli*, then as *Cedgueli* (*c.* 1150) and as *Kedwely* (1191). We do not know who Cadwal was, but the **-i** in Cedweli indicates 'territory belonging to', and was commonly used of 'territory belonging to the descendants of' the person named. At first, it referred to the commote of Cedweli and then later to the town. The tendency has been for the name to be pronounced as in the modern Welsh variant Cydweli which is reflected in the anglicized Kidwelly observed from at least the 15th century (*Kydwelly*, 1458; *kydweli*, 1566).

DEGANNWY   Caern
'the Decantae'

Early Latin references (812) record the town as '*Arx Decantorum*' 'the town of the Decantae', a British tribe who would have called the town something like 'Decantoviom' which became *Dugannu* (1191) and *Diganwy* (1254). In medieval Welsh texts the tribe is referred to as Dygant, and the town of Degannwy as Dygant or Caer Ddygant. Degannwy is the recommended spelling on linguistic grounds, although Deganwy persists in modern usage.

DEINIOLEN   Caern

The original name of this village near the Dinorwig quarry was Ebeneser, from the name of the Nonconformist chapel there. At the beginning of the 20th century Ebeneser was replaced by Deiniolen, a name coined from the parish name Llanddeiniolen, the **llan** commemorating the saint Deiniolen. He was the son of Deiniol of Bangor whom he succeeded as abbot. His name contains the diminutive ending **-en**, 'little Deiniol'; he was also known as Deiniolfab, 'son of Deiniol'. Two churches were founded by Deiniolen, one at Llan-ddaniel Fab in Anglesey, the other at Llanddeiniolen.

DENBIGH see DINBYCH

DINBYCH   DENBIGH   Denb
'little fort'
din 'fortress stronghold', **bych (bach)** 'small'

The original 'little fort' (*Dinbych*, 1269) was a castle built three-quarters of a mile south of the present Denbigh in the northern corner of the commote of Cinmerch *c.* 1230 when Llywelyn ap Iorwerth granted the land to his daughter Gwenllian. The mound-castle was known for a long time as Llys Gwenllian (**llys** 'court'), and also as Hen Ddinbych (**hen** 'old'). In 1283, Edward 1 ordered the building of the new castle and town of the present, larger, Denbigh (*Dynebegh*, 1311). In the anglicized spelling **-gh** did actually represent the Welsh **-ch** and was pronounced **-ch** in Welsh and in English (as in Gough, a spelling of Goch 'the red one'). In time the **gh** disappeared as in other English words (such as **bough** and **through** and Vaughan for Fychan 'the small one') to give a modern anglicized pronunciation of 'Denby'. Compare Tenby in Pembrokeshire which comes from another Dinbych.

DINBYCH-Y-PYSGOD   TENBY   Pemb
'the little fort of the fish' 'the little fort'
din 'fort', **bych**(**an**) 'small', **y** 'the', **pysgod** 'fish'

The Welsh and English place-names are identical in origin to those of Dinbych and Denbigh in Denbighshire, with the 'little fort' here being located at the site of the 13th-century Tenby Castle (*Dinbych*, *c.* 1275; *Tynebegh* 1292). The qualifying **y pysgod** (*Dinbych y pysgod*, 1566; *Tenby y piscoid*, 1586) is a reference to its importance as a fishing port with its daily fish-market. The change to Tenby (1482) certainly reflects the fact that the **-gh-** was no longer pronounced but could possibly also be influenced by Viking names ending in **by**. The change from **D-** to **T-** is more difficult to explain. Perhaps it was influenced by the regular interchange of **-t-** and **-d-** at the beginning of words in Welsh.

DISERTH   DYSERTH   Flints
'hermitage, retreat'
diserth 'hermit's cell'

The Latin **desertum** was used in the Early Church for the cell used by a hermit or as a retreat. This gave rise to Dysart in Fife, and to several place-names in Ireland (such as Disert, Desert and Dysert) and in Wales (such as Diserth near Builth and Dyserth near Welshpool). The Diserth in Flintshire occurs in the Domesday Book (1086) as *Dissard*. The variant with **-y-** rather than the historically more correct **-i-** has been in use for a long time (*Dyssart*, 1320) and is today the more commonly used spelling. Dyserth has been strongly influenced by the perception that Dyserth comprised the intensive prefix **dy** and **serth** 'steep', since Dyserth is below one of the steeper slopes of Moel Hiraddug.

DOLGARROG   Caern
'the water-meadow of the wild stream'
dôl 'water-meadow', meadow', **carrog** 'torrent, fast-flowing stream'

The water-meadows are between the river Conwy, Afon Porth-llwyd and Afon Ddu. There is an escarpment here down which several streams tumble to the meadows beside the river Conwy. On the nearby river Dulyn is a waterfall and at Dolgarrog itself there was a hydro-electric scheme. Although it appears in 1534 as Dolgarrog the 1666 reference to *Dole y Garrog* suggests that the earliest form was probably 'Dôl y Garrog' (**y** 'the').

DOLGELLAU   Mer
'the water-meadow of cells'
dôl 'water-meadow, meadow', **cellau** (plural of **cell**) 'cells'

Originally, **dôl** meant 'bend in a river' and then later it came to refer to the land enclosed within that loop, hence 'water-meadow' and then simply 'meadow'. Dolgellau (*Dolkelew*, 1254) is at the confluence of the rivers Wnion and Aran. The precise significance of **cellau** is obscure. The reference is possibly to monastic cells, but a stronger case could be made for merchants' stalls or booths.

DOWLAIS   Glam
'black brook'
du 'black', **glais** 'brook'

A brook could be described as black because of muddy waters or a dark river-bed or because it was shaded in certain

34

parts. Other rivers (in Carmarthenshire and Glamorgan) are similarly called Dulais, but in Dowlais (and others such as Dywlais, Dywlas and Diwlas) there seems to have been an early development of **du-** to **dyw-**. The word **glais** for a brook, as seen in Morlais and Gwynlais as well as in the name of the village Y Glais (*Aber Gleys*, 1203), seems to occur mainly in south Wales.

DWYGYFYLCHI   Caern
'two circular fortresses'
dwy 'two', **cyfylchi** 'circular fortress'

Early forms are *Dwy Kyuelchy* (1284), *Dwygyvylchi* (1413) and *Y ddwy gyfylchi* (16th cent.). The word **cyfylchi** appears almost exclusively in place-names to signify a circular strong-hold or fortress; other examples are in Glamorgan and Monmouthshire. There are several fortifications on the surrounding hills.

EBBW VALE   GLYNEBWY   Monm
'valley of the (river) Ebwy'
glyn 'valley'

The river-name was originally Ebwydd (*Eboth*, 1101–20) which is made up of **eb-** 'horse' (as in the modern Welsh **ebol** 'colt') and either **gwyth** 'anger', or **gŵydd** 'wild' or simply the suffix **-wydd**. The reference to horses may be to those who habitually drank from it or, as is more likely, to the nature of the river, a descriptive reference reinforced by at least two of the possible second elements, 'angry horse river' or 'wild horse river'. In time, Ebwydd became Ebwy (as in Glynebwy) and then Ebw (as in Ebbw Vale). The industrial town of Ebbw Vale developed around the iron-works which were established in 1786 at the farm at Pen-y-cae ('top of the field') near the source of the river. Indeed, the settlement was called

Pen-y-cae until the name Ebbw Vale was imposed as an artificial creation in the 19th century. Glynebwy is a translation of Ebbw Vale.

Y FALI see **VALLEY**

Y FELINHELI Caern
'the sea-mill'
y 'the', **melin** 'mill', **heli** 'brine, salt-water, sea'

There are several mills in the area dependent on the tidal power of the Menai Strait. During the late 18th century the Dinorwig quarries built an extensive harbour for the export of slate, which was transported to the quay on a purpose-built narrow gauge railway. It was this industrial expansion which gave Y Felinheli (*Felin-hely*, 1838) the alternative name of Port Dinorwig or Port Dinorwic (*the port of Dinorwic*, 1851). The demise of the slate industry and the development of the harbour for recreational sailing has recently caused the community to consider the name Port Dinorwig as redundant.

Y FENNI see **ABERGAFENNI**

FFESTINIOG see **BLAENAU FFESTINIOG**

FISHGUARD   ABERGWAUN Pemb
'fish yard, yard for catching or keeping fish' 'mouth of the river Gwaun'
Scandinavian **fiskr** 'fish', **garthr** 'yard', Welsh **aber** 'estuary'

The earliest form of Fishguard (*Fissigart*, 1200) points to the Scandinavians. Several place-names on the Pembrokeshire coast have Scandinavian origins and have survived partly because, as in this case, the Scandinavian words resembled

English words in sound and meaning. However, the Welsh name Abergwaun was in parallel use (*Fissegard, id est, Aber gweun*, 1210). The river-name Gwaun means 'marsh, moor'.

FLINT   (Y FFLINT)   Flints
'hard rock, flint'

In medieval English **flint** meant 'hard rock' rather than having today's strict geological sense. The castle at Flint (*le Flynt*, 1277) was built on a stony platform jutting into the river Dee. This was 'the rock' which explains the definite article appearing in the earlier forms (*le Fflynt*, 1300; *y flynt*, 14th cent.) and even in the French translation (*Le Chaylou*, 1277; *Le Cayllou*, 1278). The French name did not survive any more than did the definite article in English. In Welsh, however, despite **flint** being an English word, it is customary to refer to the town as Y Fflint and to the county as Sir y Fflint.

Y GELLI GANDRYLL see HAY-ON-WYE

GLYNEBWY see EBBW VALE

GLYN-NEATH   GLYN-NEDD   Glam
'the narrow valley of the (river) Nedd, Neath'
glyn 'narrow valley'

Slightly to the north of this narrow valley (*Glynneth*, 1281; *Glyn Nedd*, 15th cent.) the rivers Pyrddin and Mellte join the river Neath. A little lower down the river the valley opens out to the Vale of Neath.

GOWERTON   TRE-GŴYR   Glam
'the town of the Gower (peninsula)'
English -**ton** 'town', Welsh **tre** 'town'

The older name was Gower Road Station (1860), which then
became Gower Road, because of its location on one of the
main routes into the Gower peninsula and through which the
railway from Swansea to Llanelli ran. In 1886 the developing
town was dignified with a new 'town' name in English. Much
later this was translated into Welsh as Tre-gŵyr (showing its
late provenance because the more correct Welsh form would
have been 'Tre-ŵyr' or 'Tref-ŵyr'). Gower or Gŵyr (**gŵyr**
'curved') was originally the name of an extensive commote
(of which the peninsula was only a small part) whose general
shape was curved; others have argued that the distinctive
hook-like shape of the peninsula gave its name to the
commote.

GRESFORD   GRESFFORDD   Denb
'grassy ford'
Old English **græs** 'grass', **ford** 'ford'

The place-name appears in the Domesday Book (1086) in an
incorrect form *Gretford* and regularly (from 1273) as
Gresford (although a *Grassford* does appear in 1399). There
was a ford here through the river Alun (probably where the
Gresford Bridge is today) which, it would seem, was
characterized by a notably grassy approach. It is highly
unlikely that the ford itself would have been grassy
underfoot, even in very dry weather. In company with other
place-names in the area the Welsh Gresffordd (*Yngressffordd*,
16th cent.; *Gresfordh, c.* 1700) reveals a modification to the
Welsh **ffordd** 'road, way' (which is itself a borrowing from
Old English **ford**).

Y GROESLON   Caern
(the) 'cross-road'
(**y** 'the'), **croes** 'cross', **lôn** 'road'

At Y Groeslon (1798; *Croes-lôn*, 1838) the road from Carmel
to Llandwrog crosses the major road from Caernarfon to
Porthmadog.

GRONANT   Flints
'the gravel-brook' or ' gravel-valley'
gro 'gravel, shingle', **nant** 'stream, brook' or 'dingle, valley'

The name is very well attested as Gronant from the
Domesday Book (1086) onwards, but it is difficult to be sure
whether the shingle was a characteristic of a brook or of a
narrow valley (since **nant** carries both meanings). Many
medieval records also refer to *Gronantesmore* (e.g. 1348);
'moor' here means 'marshland', the extensive tracts of marsh
from Ffynnongroyw to Rhyl.

GWALCHMAI   Angl
'(the township of) Gwalchmai'

Gwalchmai ap Meilir (1130–80), one of the medieval court
poets, gave his name to the township in Malltraeth called
Trewalchmai (*Trefwalkemyth*, 1291–2; *Trefwalghmey*, 1350)
(**tref** 'township') which became simply Gwalchmai
(*Gwalghmey*, 1352).

HARLECH   Mer
'fine rock'
hardd 'fine, fair', **llech** 'rock, slab'

Harlech was in existence well before the 13th-century

Norman castle came to be built on the prominent crag here and before the name was first recorded as in the anglicized form of *Hardelagh* (1290–2). The **-dd-** was lost in Welsh pronunciation (*Harlech*, 14th cent.) but survived a little longer in some texts (*Harddlech*, 1450).

HAVERFORDWEST   HWLFFORDD   Pemb
'western goat ford'
Old English **hæfer** 'he-goat, buck', **ford** 'ford', **west** 'west'

The river (Western) Cleddau is apparently still fordable at low tide. At one time goats may have habitually been seen near this ford. The place-name is first recorded as *Haverfordia* (*c.* 1191) and later in such forms as *Hareford* (1283) and *Hereford alias Hareforde* (1385). It was this potential confusion with the Hereford in England which prompted the addition of the distinguishing West (as in *Heverford West*, 1448 and *Herefordwest*, 1471). The Welsh form Hwlffordd (*Hawlffordd*, 14th cent.; *Hwlffordd*, 15th cent.) is a development of the early English forms (still heard as Harford locally) with **-r-** becoming **-l-** (as with **maenor** becoming **maenol**) and **-d** becoming **-dd** (as in several place-names such as Gresford and Gresffordd, Whitford and Chwitffordd and in the English word **ford** itself, which became Welsh **ffordd** 'road, way').

HAWARDEN   PENARLÂG   Flints
'high enclosure' 'headland, height rich in cattle'
Old English **hēah** 'high', **worðign** 'enclosure', Welsh **pennardd** 'high ground', **alafog** 'rich in cattle'

Both English and Welsh names refer to the prominent position of the castle and village above the Dee plain. The English form appears in the Domesday Book of 1086 as *Haordine* and from about the 16th century Hawarden has been pronounced as Harden, the usual English pronunciation, and until the last century under Welsh influence as three-syllable Hawarden (*Harden otherwise Howarden*, 1839). This explains the discrepancy between the modern pronunciation and spelling. The Welsh name Penarlâg was in existence long before the English name but is not recorded until the early 14th century (as *Pennardlaawc* and *Penardlaoc*). **Alafog** or **alaog** comes from **alaf** 'cattle', although it has been argued that Alaog could be a personal name.

HAY-ON-WYE   Y GELLI GANDRYLL   Brec

'enclosed forest' 'woodland divided into many plots'
Old English **hæg** 'enclosed forest', Welsh **y** 'the', **celli** 'woodland', **candryll** 'a hundred plots'

Forest areas were often fenced to provide hunting grounds; this one was a very early enclosure (*Hagan*, 958; *Haya*, 1144). The reference to its location on the river Wye is modern. The Welsh name Y Gelli appears much later (*i'r Gelli, c.* 1450; *Y Gelli*, 1566) but has the same woodland connotations. Later still, the qualifying Gandryll was added (*Gelli gandrell*, 1614) but the exact significance has been lost leading to some speculation. **Candryll** probably comprises **cant** 'a hundred' and **dryll** 'piece' and usually means 'shattered', 'in a hundred pieces', which is difficult to relate to woodland. However, **dryll** is also used of a small piece or plot of land, so **candryll** could indicate that the former woodland had been cleared and divided into a hundred (or many) plots of land.

HEN-DŶ-GWYN AR DAF see WHITLAND

HIRWAUN   Glam

'long moor'
hir 'long', **gwaun** 'moor, mountain pasture'

The extensive moorland is to the south-west of Hirwaun and

41

Pen-y-waun. It was also known as *Hirwaun Wrgan* (1638), a reference to Gwrgan, reputedly the last king of Glamorgan, who is said to have given the common land to the freeholders of the manor of Miskin and Glyn Rhondda. Early forms are *Hyrweunworgan* (1203) and *Hirwen Urgan* (1536–9).

HÔB, YR see HOPE

HOLT   Denb
'wood'
Old English **holt** 'wood'

There are two settlements on either side of the river Dee, Farndon on the English side, Holt on the Welsh side. Holt may have been the area which provided timber or hunting for the castle at Holt. It was frequently referred to not only as Holt (*Holte*, 1326) but as The Holt (*the holt*, 1535) and it appears in Welsh documents as *yr holt, c.* 1566. In addition, a further name, Lyons, seems to have been used regularly, a name which emerged in the Middle Ages (*Castrum Leonis*, 1316; *the castle of Leouns*, 1346; *the castle of Lyons lately called the castle of le Holt*, 1347) and would seem to mean 'castle of the lion', which was translated into Welsh as Llys y Llewod (*lyselawod*, 1431 'the court of the lions'). However, the general belief is that the medieval form is an adaptation of *Castra Legionis* 'fort of the legion', referring to the Twentieth Legion which had its base at Chester (also referred to as *Castra Legionum*) and which manufactured its tiles at Holt.

HOLYHEAD   CAERGYBI   Angl
'holy headland'   'the fort of Cybi'
Old English **hālig** 'holy', **hēafod** 'headland', Welsh **caer** 'fort'

Holyhead is on an island called Holy Island or Ynys Gybi

('Cybi's island'), and the monastic settlement associated with the 6th-century St Cybi is common to the English and Welsh place-names. In Holyhead (*Haliheved*, 1315; *Holiheved*, 1322; *Le Holyhede*, 1394; *Holyhede*, 1395), the headland is actually Holyhead Mountain (Mynydd Twr 'cairn mountain') in the north-west of Holy Island. In Caergybi (*Castro Kyby*, 1291; *Castelkyby*, 1310; *kaer gybi*, 1566) the church of St Cybi is within the Roman fort. Translations of **caer** as *castrum* and *castle* commonly occur in place-names in legal or other documents; they had no life outside the scribe's usage.

HOLYWELL   TREFFYNNON   Flints
'holy well' 'village of the well'
Old English **hālig** 'holy', **wella** 'well', Welsh **tref** 'town', **ffynnon** 'well, spring'

According to a legend of the 7th-century Gwenfrewi (anglicized as Winifred) was beheaded by a rejected suitor. Her head rolled down a hill towards Beuno's chapel and a spring burst forth where the head stopped (*Haliwell*, 1093). St Beuno, her uncle, restored her head and a nunnery (with Winifred as abbess) was established around St Winifred's Well (Ffynnon Wenfrewi). The well's curative waters make it a centre of pilgrimage to this day. In Welsh, the name of the town appears as *Treffynnon* in 1329.

HOPE   YR HÔB   Flints
'enclosed land in a marsh'
Old English **hop** 'enclosed land especially in waste land or marsh'

Hope is on fairly dry land beside the river Alun. The place-name in English (*Hope*, 1086) reflects the Mercian settlement of the area but its naturalization in a Welsh form (*Hob*, 1580; *Yr Hôb*, *c.* 1700) is evidence of the restricted English influence in the Middle Ages and early modern period. *Queen's Hope* (1398) and *Hope Regine* (1430) were also used at one time, commemorating the fact that Edward I, after accepting the surrender of the nearby Caergwrle Castle, presented the castle and much of the parish to his wife Eleanor.

HWLFFORDD see **HAVERFORDWEST**

KIDWELLY see **CYDWELI**

KILGETTY see **CILGETI**

KINMEL see **CINMEL**

KNIGHTON   TREFYCLO   Radn
'farm of the followers', 'farm by the dyke'
Old English **cniht** 'personal followers', **tūn** 'farm' Welsh **tref** 'farm', **y** 'the', **clawdd** 'dyke'

Knighton appears in the Domesday Book of 1086 as *Chenistetone* and more recognizably in 1193 as *Cnicheton*; the Old English word **cniht** (which developed into modern English **knight**) meant 'personal followers, young men, servants'. In much the same way, the word **tūn**, which became modern English **town**, had an earlier meaning of 'farm' and it appears as **-ton** at the end of very many English place-names. Trefyclo has also undergone changes in form and meaning. Like **tūn**, **tref** originally meant 'farm' before emerging as the modern Welsh word for 'town'. The farm was adjacent to Offa's Dyke (Clawdd Offa) hence Trefyclawdd (as in *Treficlaudh*, 1586). The stress originally fell on **clawdd** but then shifted to the more usual Welsh position of last syllable but one, which had the effect of reducing **-clawdd** to **-clo**. This appears to have happened early on (*Trebuclo*, 1536–9).

44

LAMPETER see **LLANBEDR PONT STEFFAN**

LAUGHARNE   TALACHARN   Carm
'the end of -'
tâl 'the end of'

Talacharn (*Talacharn*, 1191) was the name of the commote
and lordship. The first element **tâl** 'end' is evident enough but
the **-acharn** is obscure, although attempts have been made to
link it with the name of the brook Coran. The site of the
castle was actually called Abercoran (*Abercorran*, 1191) (**aber**
'mouth of the brook'). Lacharn was used of the town (an
abbreviation of *Castell Talacharn*). Laugharne is an anglicized spelling with **-gh-** representing the Welsh **-ch-**, but in
today's anglicized pronunciation is 'Larne'.

LLANANDRAS see **PRESTEIGNE**

LLANBADARN FAWR   Card
'the principal church of (St) Padarn'
llan 'church', **mawr** 'big'

There are eight place-names carrying dedications to St
Padarn (including another Llanbadarn Fawr in Radnor-
shire). This church near Aberystwyth was the principal
church in the area. It was founded by the 5th–6th-century St
Padarn who was abbot and bishop there. Tradition has it
that Padarn visited Jerusalem with St David and St Teilo.
Early forms are *Lampadervaur* (1181–2) and *Llanbadarn
Vawr* (1557).

LLANBEDR PONT STEFFAN   LAMPETER   Card
'church of (St) Pedr by Stephen's bridge' 'church of (St) Peter'
llan 'church', **pont** 'bridge'

The Welsh name of the church was Llanbedr (*Lanpeder* 1284) from **llan** and Pedr ('Peter'). The English name is an anglicization not only of **llan** but of the saint's name. Interestingly, the change to **-m-** in Lampeter faithfully reflects the local Welsh pronunciation as 'Llambed'. The need to distinguish this church of Llanbedr from other churches dedicated to St Peter gave rise to *Lampeder Talpont* (1303–4) 'at the end of the bridge' (where **tâl** means 'end of'), *Lampeder tal pont stevyn* (1407) and *Lampeter Pount Steune* (1301). Stephen was probably a Norman with responsibility for maintaining the bridge.

LLANBERIS   Caern
'church of (St) Peris'
llan 'church'

The church is dedicated to St Peris (*Lanperis*, 1283), and although he is traditionally associated with two churches in Caernarfonshire there is very little to indicate that he was a Welsh saint. He lived sometime between the 11th and 12th centuries. The church is in the hamlet called Nant Peris, and the name is also preserved in the associated Afon Nant Peris which flows from Snowdon's Pen y Pass to Llyn Peris. Another hamlet at Coed y Ddôl on the shores of Llyn Padarn, and adjacent Castell Dolbadarn, developed rapidly during the expansion of the Dinorwig quarry. Although the church in this larger village was dedicated to St Padarn, the parish name Llanberis gravitated away from Nant Peris so that the village at Coed y Ddôl came to be recognized as Llanberis. On some maps Nant Peris is also shown as Old Llanberis but this has no local currency.

46

LLANDDEWI BREFI   Card
'church of (St) Dewi on the (river) Brefi'
llan 'church'

There are some fifteen place-names with church dedications
to Dewi. This Llanddewi (*Landewi Brevi*, 13th cent.) is on the
river Brefi, which rises at Blaen Brefi (**blaen** 'headwater')
between Cwm Berwyn and Esgair Llethr and flows past
Llanddewi Brefi into the river Teifi. The river-name probably
derives from **bref** 'a roar, a bellow', alluding to a wild, noisy
river. Legend maintains that at the Convocation of Brefi,
Dewi roared forth his accusations against heretics with a
voice like a trumpet.

LLANDDEWI NANT HODDNI   LLANTHONY   Monm
'church of (St) Dewi on the river Hoddni'
llan 'church', **nant** 'river, brook'

The river Hoddni rises on the Hay Bluff and flows through
the Vale of Ewyas past Llanthony and into the river Monnow
at Allt-yr-Ynys. The name Hoddni derives from **hawdd** 'easy,
pleasant, quiet', an element found in a number of river-names
(such as Hoddnant). In some of these names, Hoddni became
Honddu (reinforced by the association with **du** 'black'), as in
Aberhonddu, Brecon. However, in the name Llanddewi Nant
Hoddni (*Landewi Nanthotheni*, 13th cent.) several middle
syllables were unusually lost to give Llanthony (*Lantony*,
1160–80). An alternative and perhaps preferable explanation
is that **nant** in Nant Hoddni was supplanted by **llan** to give
'Llanthoddni' which became Llanthoni with the **-t-** being the
remains of Nant-. The existence of Llanthony Priory testifies
to the tranquillity of the river and valley, as do several
documents related to other Hoddni rivers, especially the Glyn
Hoddnant in Pembs where Dewi established his monastery of
Tyddewi (St Davids).

47

LLANDDULAS   Denb
'church (on the river) Dulas'
llan 'church'

The church of Llanddulas (*Llan Dhylas, c.* 1700) is located
beside the river Dulas (1504). The first element in the river-
name is certainly **du** 'black', perhaps because of murky dark
waters, or because it was in shadow or overgrown in parts.
The second element is probably **glas** 'blue' but could possibly
be **glas, glais** 'stream' which however tends to occur in south
Wales (as in Dulais and Dowlais).

LLANDEGFAN   Angl
'church of (St) Tegfan'
llan 'church'

The earliest records have *Llandegvan* (1254). Very little is
known of St Tegfan except that he was a confessor in St
Cybi's monastery in Caergybi (Holyhead), probably in the
6th century.

LLANDEILO   Carm
'church of (St) Teilo'
llan 'church'

Many references (such as *Lanteliau Mawr*, 1130; *Llandilo
Vawr*, 1656) include the distinguishing **mawr** 'great' since this
church was one of the earliest to be dedicated to St Teilo, the
6th-century saint who is said to have visited Jerusalem with
St David and St Padarn. Many churches are dedicated to him
in south Wales and in Brittany.

LLANDOVERY see LLANYMDDYFRI

LLANDRILLO-YN-RHOS see RHOS-ON-SEA

LLANDRINDOD (WELLS) Radn
'church of the Trinity'
llan 'church', **trindod** 'trinity'

The original name of the church was Llanddwy (*Lando*, 1291) 'church of God' (*Dwyw*, God). The dedication to the Trinity (*Llandrindod*, 1554–8) came later. Wells was added to draw attention to the 19th-century exploitation of the chalybeate springs in the spa town.

LLANDUDNO Caern
'church of (St) Tudno'
llan 'church'

The earliest records have *Llandudno* (1291) and *Lantudenou* (1376). This is the only church dedicated to this 6th-century saint of whom little is known.

LLANDYSUL Card
'church of (St) Tysul'
llan 'church'

Recorded in 1291 as *Landessel* and in 1299 as *Lantissill*. Very little is known about this saint. Another church is dedicated to him in Montgomeryshire and in Brittany where he was celebrated as a bishop.

LLANELLI Carm
'church of (St) Elli'
llan 'church'

The church is recorded in 1160–85 as *Lann elli*. Elli was reputedly one of the daughters of 5th-century prince Brychan.

LLANFAIR CAEREINION   Mont
'church of (St) Mary in Caereinion'
llan 'church'

The early references are to the church of St Mary (as in
Llanveyr, 1254), but the fairly common dedication to St Mary
required further qualification (*Llanvair in Krynion*, 1579;
Llanvaire in Kerynion 1596–7), by denoting the name of the
cantref Caereinion (*Keiriniaun*, 1263), the fort of Einion (**caer**
'fort').

LLANFAIRFECHAN   Caern
'the little church of (St) Mary'
bechan 'little'

The common occurrence of churches dedicated to St Mary
(*Lanueyr*, 1284; *Llanvayar*, 1291) necessitated an added
qualifier, which distinguished this church of St Mary
(*Llanvair Vechan*, 1475) from the larger church of St Mary at
Conwy some five miles away.

LLANFAIR-YM-MUALLT see BUILTH

LLANFAIR PWLLGWYNGYLL   Angl
'the church of (St) Mary in Pwllgwyngyll'
llan 'church', **pwll** 'pool', **gwyn** 'white', **cyll** plural of **collen**
'hazel'

The church overlooks an inlet in the Menai Strait. The
popularity of churches called Llanfair necessitated a defin-
ing location, in this case the township of Pwllgwyngyll (*Llan
Vair y pwll Gwinghill*, 1536–9; *ll.fair ymhwll gwingill*, 1566).
There is documentary evidence of white hazel in the vicinity.
The internationally celebrated addition to the name
-gogerychwyrndrobwll-llantysiliogogogoch is little more than
a fanciful tag deliberately coined to ensure prominence for a

temporary railway station and freight yard which was about to become redundant following completion of the Britannia Bridge in 1850. A tailor from Menai Bridge is credited with the fabrication, which is based on features in the nearby landscape. The following elements are identifiable: **go-ger** 'fairly close to', **y** 'the', **chwyrn** 'wild', **trobwll** 'whirlpool' (the turbulent and treacherous Swillies near the Menai Bridge), **llantysilio** 'church of (St) Tysilio' (the church of Llandysilio on Ynys Tysilio in the Menai Strait near Menai Bridge), Llandysiliogogo was the name of a parish in Cardiganshire, **coch** 'red' (alluding to Ynys Gorad Goch, the island in the Menai Strait). How he came to incorporate a Cardiganshire parish is not known, unless it evolved from an earlier attempt at something like 'Llandysilio-Gorad-Goch'.

LLANFIHANGEL-AR-ARTH   Card
'church of (St) Mihangel on the high hill'
llan 'church', **gor** 'exceedingly', **garth** 'wooded slope, hill'

Forty-five place-names in Wales have churches dedicated to Mihangel (Michael the archangel). This church was originally called *Llanfihangel Orarth* (1291), where Orarth is **gor** 'exceedingly' and **garth** 'a hill or a wooded slope'. In time the alternative Llanfihangel Iorath emerged (influenced by Iorath or Yorath, a variant of Iorwerth) and is still recognized today.

LLANFYLLIN   Mont
'church of (St) Myllin(g)'
llan 'church'

The early forms seem to alternate between Myllin and Mylling (*Llanvelig* 1254, *Lanvyllyn* 1291, *Lanvethlyng* 1309). The 7th-century saint was Irish (with variants in Moling, Mullin and Mulling) and is not known to have actually visited Wales.

LLANGADOG   Carm
'church of (St) Cadog'
llan 'church'

Llangadog has been the usual form (*Lancadauc*, 1281;
Lankadoc, 1284), but occasionally **mawr** 'great' was added
(*Ll. Cadog Fawr*, 1590) to distinguish it from fifteen other
churches dedicated to the 6th-century St Cadog (occasionally
appearing as St Catwg) who also founded the church at
Llancarfan.

LLANGEITHO   Card
'church of (St) Ceithio'
llan 'church'

It is likely that Ceithio is an Irish form of the Welsh personal
name Ceidio found in place-names, for example Rhodogeidio
in Anglesey and Ceidio in Caernarfonshire and in the river-
name Ceidio or Ceidiog in Merionethshire. Early forms are
Lankethau (1284) and *Langeytho* (1290). St Ceithio or Ceitho
was one of the five saints (reputedly born at one birth) to
whom Llanpumsaint is dedicated (**pump** 'five', **saint** 'saints').

LLANGEFNI   Angl
'church on the (river) Cefni'
llan 'church'

The church (*Llangevni*, 1254) is adjacent to the river Cefni
(**cafn** 'dip, hollow') but is dedicated to St Cyngar, hence the
occasional *Llangyngar* (1509).

LLANGOLLEN   Denb
'church of (St) Collen'
llan 'church'

Recorded in 1234 as *Lancollien*. Other churches in Cornwall and in Brittany are dedicated to St Collen but little else is known of this 7th-century saint.

LLANGURIG   Mont
'church of (St) Curig'
llan 'church'

The name is recorded in 1254 as *Lankiric*. The 6th-century saint's name is also found in the nearby Foel Gurig. He founded a monastery in Brittany where he was celebrated as a bishop and was buried.

LLANGYBI   Card
'church of (St) Cybi'
llan 'church'

An early form is *Lankeby* (1284). There are other churches dedicated to the 6th-century St Cybi, in Caernarfonshire, in Monmouthshire and in Cornwall, in addition to the monastery he founded in Caergybi (Holyhead) and where he was abbot.

LLANIDLOES   Mont
'church of (St) Idloes'
llan 'church'

Recorded in 1254 as *Lanidloes*. This is the only church dedicated to a saint of whom very little is known.

LLANILLTUD FAWR   LLANTWIT MAJOR   Glam
'the principal church of (St) Illtud'
llan 'church', Latin **major** 'major', **mawr** 'main, major'

There were three other churches dedicated to St Illtud in
Glamorgan (Llanilltud-iuxta-Neath or Llanilltud Nedd or
Llanilltud Fach, Llantwit Fardre or Llanilltud Faerdref, and
Llanilltud Gŵyr or Ilston). It was at Llantwit Major that
Illtud established a monastery in the 6th century and became
abbot there. Early forms are *Landiltuit* (1106), *Lannyltwyt*
(1291), *Llanulltut* (1378–86) and the contracted *Lantwyt*
(1480) which gave rise to the 'English' Llantwit. A number of
other churches are dedicated to St Illtud in south Wales and
in Brittany.

LLANLLYFNI   Caern
'church beside the (river) Llyfni'
llan 'church'

The river Llyfni flows from Llyn Nantlle through Tal-y-sarn
and Llanllyfni (*Thlauthleueny*, 1352; *Llanllyfne*, 1432) to
enter the sea at Pontlyfni. The church is on a slight rise beside
the river. Llyfni means 'the smooth-flowing one' (**llyfn**
'smooth').

LLANNERCH-Y-MEDD   Angl
'the glade of mead'
llannerch 'glade, clearing', **medd** 'mead'

One possible explanation is that bees frequented the glade
and that their honey was used in the production of mead.
However, it is more likely that the glade was habitually the
location of convivial gatherings. Early forms are *llann'meth*
(1445–6) and *Lannerch y medd* (15th cent.).

54

LLANRUG   Caern
'the church in Rug'
llan 'church'

The full name was Llanfihangel-yn-Rug (*ll.v'el yn Ruc*, 1566;
Llanvihengle in Rug, 1614) 'the church of Mihangel (St
Michael) in (the township called) Rug' (**grug** 'heather').
However, the church was also referred to as Llanrug (*Lanruk*,
1284; *Llan Ruge*, 1535).

LLANRWST   Denb
'church of (St) Gwrwst'
llan 'church'

Recorded as *lhannruste* in 1254, as *Lannwrvst* in 1291, and as
Llanwrwst in 1398, this is the only church dedicated to this
little-known saint.

LLANSANFFRAID GLAN CONWY   Denb
'church of St Ffraid beside (the river) Conwy'
llan 'church', **sain** 'saint', **glan** 'bank, shore'

Ffraid was one of the Welsh forms of the name of the Irish
saint Brigid. (Other variants include Brid as in Saint-y-brid or
St Brides Major in Glamorgan, and Ffrêd as in Sain Ffrêd in
Pembrokeshire.) It is common in Welsh for the word for
'saint' to lose **-t**, as in Sain Ffagan, Sain Tathan (St Athan),
and Llan Sain Siôr (St George, Abergele). Some dozen
parishes are called Llansanffraid with or without further
locational qualification. Llansanffraid (*Llansanfraid*, 1535;
Lhan St Ffraid, *c.* 1700) was used regularly until Llansanffraid Glan Conwy (*Llan Sanfraed Glan Conwy*, 1713)
emerged. Today, there is a tendency to refer to the village
simply as Glan Conwy.

LLANSANFFRAID GLYNCEIRIOG   Denb
'church of (St) Ffraid in the valley of the (river) Ceiriog'
llan 'church', **sain** 'saint', **glyn** 'narrow valley'

See the previous entry for Ffraid. Early forms (*Lansanfreit*, 1291) were supplemented by a locational qualification referring to the narrow valley (*llansanffraid y glyn*, 1560; *ll.sain ffred glyn Kerioc*, 1566; *Lansantffraid Glynn Ceiriog* 1795). The village is more commonly referred to as Glynceiriog. Confusion with the more generally known Dyffryn Ceiriog (**dyffryn** 'valley') is unlikely since **glyn** denotes the much narrower valley at this point. Other names which record the river-name are Llanarmon Dyffryn Ceiriog, Tregeiriog and Chirk.

LLANSAWEL   (1)   Carm
'church of (St) Sawyl'
llan 'church'

Early forms are *Lansawyl* (1265) and *Lansawel* (1301). Llansewyl is also used occasionally. The 6th-century saint's name is a variant of Samuel.

LLANSAWEL (2) see **BRITON FERRY**

LLANTHONY see **LLANDDEWI NANT HODDNI**

LLANTRISANT   Glam
'church of three saints'
llan 'church', **tri** 'three', **sant** 'saint'

The three saints of Llantrisant (*Landtrissen*, 1246) are Dyfodwg, Gwynno and Illtud.

LLANTWIT MAJOR see **LLANILLTUD FAWR**

LLANWRDA   Carm
'church of (St) Gwrdaf'
llan 'church'

An early form is *Llanwrdaf* (1302–3). This is the only church
dedicated to Gwrdaf, who does not appear in any pedigree of
Welsh saints and of whom nothing is known.

LLANWRTYD (WELLS)   Brec
'church of Gwrtud'
llan 'church'

The name occurs in 1553 as *Llanwrtid* and in 1566 as
Ll. Wrtyd. The modern place-name would be more correctly
spelt 'Llanwrtud' to conform with the unknown *Gwrtud*, who
was probably not a saint. The church itself is dedicated to St
David. Llanwrtyd Wells, which developed as a spa town in
the 19th century, is more than a mile away from the village of
Llanwrtyd.

LLANYBYDDER   Carm
'church of the deaf (ones)'
llan 'church', **byddair** plural of **byddar** 'deaf'

Why this particular congregation (or clergy) should have
been deemed 'deaf' is a mystery. Early forms are *Lannabedeir*
(1319) and *Llanybyddeyr* (1401).

LLANYMDDYFRI   LLANDOVERY   Carm
'church near the waters'
llan 'church', **am** 'near', **dyfri** (from **dwfr**) 'waters'

The town is near the confluences of the rivers Brân,
Gwydderig and Towy. The early forms include **am** as in

Llanamdewri 12th cent., and *Lanandeveri* 1194, which later became **-ym-** (*Lanymdevery*, 1383). The **-ym-** has been lost in the local pronunciation Llandyfri which has been anglicized to Llandovery.

LOUGHOR   CASLLWCHWR   Glam
'the castle on the river Llwchwr'
cas 'castle'

The river Loughor has its source on the south-west slopes of the Black Mountain between Llandeilo and Brynaman. It flows through Cwmllwchwr (**cwm** 'valley') and is joined by the river Aman at Ammanford to enter the sea at Loughor. The castle (*gastell llychwr*, 1375–80; *Castell Logher*, 1543) was built overlooking the estuary (*chastell aber llychwr*, 1375–80, **aber** 'river-mouth'). The modern form displays **cas**, a variant of **castell** (*Caslougher*, 1691; *Câs Lychür*, 1719), with the 'English' form retaining the river-name only. The meaning of Loughor is 'the bright river' (**llychwr** 'day-light', 'brightness').

MACHEN   Monm
'land belonging to Cein'
ma 'plain, low-lying ground'

The identity of Cein or Cain is unknown but there are records from the 12th century (*Mahhayn*, 1102). Machen is beside the river Rhymni.

MACHYNLLETH   Mont
'the plain of Cynllaith'
ma 'plain, low-lying ground'

The 'low-lying land' was probably the land between the

present town and the river Dyfi (Dovey). Early forms are *Machenleyd* (1254) and *Machynllaith* (1385), but the identity of Cynllaith is unknown. The 17th-century antiquarian Camden believed that Machynlleth derived from Maglona which was actually the name of the Roman fort in Carlisle, an erroneous view which established itself in many popular books.

MAENORBŶR MANORBIER   Pemb
'the manor of Pŷr'
English **manor** 'manor', Welsh **maenor** 'manor, division of a commote'

Very little is known about Pir or Pŷr. The same name is certainly found in Ynys Bŷr (Caldy Island) a few miles west; it may have been the same person. Although modern Manorbier is a village, it was originally a division of a commote (*Mainaur pir,* 1136–54) and even described as the commote itself (*kymwt Maenawrbir, c.* 1400, **cwmwd** 'commote'), suggesting that it was an old and important centre. The place-name became anglicized by the 14th century (*Manerbire*, 1331).

MAENTWROG   Mer
'the rock of (St) Twrog'
maen 'rock, stone'

The church was dedicated to the 6th-century Twrog. An early form is *Mayntwroc* (1292–3). The stone at the south-west corner of the church is traditionally said to mark the saint's grave having been thrown there by the saint from the top of Moelwyn (or, in another version, by a giant called Twrog).

MAES-TEG   Glam
'fair field'
maes 'field', **teg** 'fair'

Maes-teg was originally the name of a farm which was
divided into three parts. In 1543 only one part *Maes tege issa*
(**issa** 'lower') happens to be recorded, but by 1630 the three
parts appear in documents: *maesteg issa, maesteg kenol* (**canol**
'middle') and *maesteg ycha* (**ucha** 'upper'). At one time the
area was called Llwyni (*y llwyney*, 1631) (**llwyni** plural of
llwyn 'bush'), but when the Maesteg Ironworks was opened
in 1826 on the site of the farm, Maes-teg was extended to be
the name of the industrial town associated with the
ironworks.

MANORBIER see MAENORBŶR

MELIDEN   ALLT MELYD   Flints
'hill of Melydn'
allt 'hill'

The hill (*Altmelyden, Allt Meliden, Melydyn*, 1291) on the
north of Graig Fawr was associated with an unidentified
saint Melydn. His name was eventually truncated in Welsh
through loss of the final **-n**, but was retained in English with
no reference to the hill. Occasionally there are forms with
Gallt (as in *galhd Melid, c.* 1700 and on recent signs), **gallt**
being a later development of **allt**.

MENAI BRIDGE   PORTHAETHWY   Angl
'(the town near the) Menai bridge' 'the ferry of Daethwy'
porth 'ferry'

There were several ferries across the Menai Strait. The
shortest route was to the area in Anglesey belonging to the
tribe of Daethwy, and which was called Porth-Ddaethwy,

subsequently Porthaethwy (*Porthathee*, 1291). Porthaethwy, or its local variant Y Borth, later became the name of the town. When Thomas Telford built the suspension bridge in 1826 the bridge was called Pont y Borth (*pont* 'bridge') and then Menai Bridge. In time Menai Bridge was also taken to refer to the town. The meaning of Menai (*Mene*, 11th cent.) is obscure but probably describes the strong current.

MERTHYR TUDFUL   (MERTHYR TYDFIL)   Glam
'the grave of Tudful'
merthyr 'grave of a saint'

In Welsh **merthyr** can mean 'martyr'. However, there is another meaning which is relevant here, namely the place where a saint was buried, a chapel erected over the site of the cemetery consecrated by the saint's bones. The saint need not necessarily have been a martyr. There is some doubt as to whether Tudful was a man or a woman; one tradition maintains Tudful was one of the daughters of Brychan and reputedly martyred in the 5th century. The place-name is recorded as *Merthir* in 1254 and as *Merthyr Tutuil* in the 13th century.

MILFORD HAVEN   ABERDAUGLEDDAU   Pemb
'harbour of the sandy fiord' 'the estuary of the two (rivers called) Cleddau'
Scandinavian **melr** 'sand-hill, sand bank', **fjǫrðr** 'fiord, inlet', Welsh **aber** 'estuary', **dau** 'two'

Milford is a place-name which shows evidence of Scandinavian presence. The early references are to the harbour or haven not the modern town, as in *de Milverdico portu* (in a Latin document of 1191), *Mellferth* (1207) and *Milford* (1219). Somewhat later, when the significance of **fjǫrðr** in the name had been lost, Haven was added as in *Milford Haven*

(1394). In the Welsh name, the estuary at Aberdaugleddau (*Aber Dav Gleddyf*, *Aber Dau Gleddau*, 15th cent.) has two rivers coming together, the Eastern Cleddau (Cleddau Wen) and the Western Cleddau (Cleddau Ddu). Cleddau (*Cledeu*, 1191) or Cleddyf 'sword' is one of several Welsh river-names associated with weapons or tools because they cut through the earth or because their waters shine.

MOELFRE   Angl
'bare hill'
moel 'bare', **bre** 'hill'

A considerable number of hills in Wales are described as **moel**, including Moel Siabod and the distinctive eminences of the Clwydian range (such as Moel y Parc, Moel Arthur, Moel Dywyll and Moel Fama). There are at least seven other places called Moelfre (here *Moylvry*, 1399; *Moelvre*, 1528–9), which contains **bre**, a relative of **bryn** 'hill' and the **brae** found in Scotland. In south Wales it occurs in Pen-bre.

MOLD   YR WYDDGRUG   Flints
'the high hill' 'the burial mound'
Norman-French **mont** 'hill', **hault** 'high', Welsh **yr** 'the', **gŵydd** 'tomb, cairn', **crug** 'mound'

The Bailey Hill near the centre of Mold may well have had a cairn of stones or a tumulus on it giving the Welsh 'Gŵydd-grug' (*Gythe Gruc*, 1280–81) which became Yr Wyddgrug. This was also the hill on which the Normans built a castle (*kastell yr wydgruc*, 14th cent.). Tracing the development of the modern name from Norman-French is difficult since many early references are in Latin documents (such as *de Monte alto*, 1267; *Montem Altum*, 1278) but the probable development was *Mont-hault* to 'Mohault' and then to Mold. There is a strong possibility that the original name was transferred from France, where there are several places called Monthaut (as happened with Montgomery).

MONMOUTH TREFYNWY   Monm
'mouth of the (river) Mynwy' 'town of Mynwy'
English **mouth** 'mouth of a river', Welsh **tref** 'town'

The river-name Mynwy (*Mynui*, *c.* 1150) was anglicized as Monnow (*Monowe*, 1567). In Welsh, the town's early name was Abermynwy (**aber** 'mouth') (*Aber Mynuy*, *c.* 1150). Its English form was 'Monnow-mouth' as in *Munwi Mutha* (11th cent.), *Munemuda* (1190), and *Monmouth* (1267). In time, Abermynwy was replaced by Trefynwy (*Tre Fynwe*, 1606). There is some doubt as to the exact meaning of Mynwy; it may signify a 'fast flowing river' (rather like Menai) or be associated with the tribe *Menapii*.

MONTGOMERY TREFALDWYN   Mont
'the town of Baldwin'
tref 'town'

The Norman lord, Roger de Montgomery, built the first castle here and named it Montgomery (*Montgomeri*, 1086) after his other castle at Montgommery in Calvados, Normandy. This castle, built at the foot of Hen Domen or Castle Hill, passed into the hands of another Norman, Baldwin de Bollers, in 1102, and eventually in 1223–4 a new castle was built on the top of the hill and called Castell Baldwin (*Kastell baldwin*, 14th. cent.) ('the castle of Baldwin'). The emerging town also took its name from Baldwin as Trefaldwyn (recorded in 1440), which gave rise to the county Sir Drefaldwyn. The change to Faldwyn from Baldwin is a regular sound-change in Welsh. However, Faldwyn was mistakenly assumed to derive from a hitherto non-existent Maldwyn, which then became a personal name and in Welsh is frequently used for the county name.

MOUNTAIN ASH   ABERPENNAR   Glam
'mouth of the (stream) Pennar'
aber 'mouth of a stream'

The stream Pennar (*Penar*, 1536–9) is named after the mountain Cefn Pennar (*cefn* 'ridge', *pennardd* 'height') and flows through Cwmpennar into the river Cynon (*Aber Pennarthe*, 1570). The 19th-century industrial development lower down the river adopted the English name Mountain Ash, allegedly at the instigation of the landowner (John Bruce Pryce) after an inn there, which was itself named after a nearby mountain ash (the rowan tree). Aberpennar was retained as the Welsh name of the town.

NANT-Y-GLO   Monm
'valley of coal (or charcoal)'
nant 'valley', **glo** 'charcoal, coal'

The name is quite common for a valley where coal was extracted or where there was a stream associated with charcoal burning. It appears in 1752 as *Nantygloe*, and in 1810 there is a reference to *Nant y glo iron works*. Coalbrookvale is an adjacent area in these upper reaches of the Ebbw Fach.

NARBERTH   ARBERTH   Pemb
'near the hedge'
yn 'at', **ar** 'near', **perth** 'hedge'

The original name of the place was, as it is in Welsh usage today, Arberth (*Arberth*, 1300–25) 'near the hedge' (in much the same way that Arfon means 'near or opposite Môn'). However, from very early on there was an alternative form, Narberth, which developed from the phrase 'yn Arberth' ('in Arberth'), with the **-n** of **yn** attaching itself to Arberth to give

'Narberth' (*Nerberth*, 1291; *la Nerbert*, 1331). (Similarly in England, Nash came from the phrase *atten ash* 'at the ash tree'.) Eventually, Narberth came to be perceived as the anglicized form of the name.

NEATH   CASTELL-NEDD   Glam
'the castle on the (river) Nedd'
castell 'castle'

Nedd and the anglicized Neath are the names of the river which the Romans recorded as Nidum and which appeared later as *Ned* (*c.* 1150), *Neth* (1191) and *Neeth* (1306). Strictly speaking the Romans used Nidum for the fort which they named after the river; this fortification also gave rise to the Welsh name Castell-nedd (*Kastell Nedd*, 1566). The exact meaning of the river-name is obscure, but it is possibly a Celtic word meaning 'shining' and related to the river Nidd in Yorkshire.

NEFYN   Caern

This village appears to have been named after an obscure person called Nefyn (*Newin*, 1254; *Nefyn*, 1291).

NEWBOROUGH   NIWBWRCH   Angl
'new borough'

In 1294, Edward I built his castle and town of Beaumaris a mile away from Llan-faes, in a deliberate attempt to weaken the power of the princes of Gwynedd by depriving them of a strategic base at Llan-faes. To appease the burgesses of Llan-faes, he established a 'new borough' (*Novus Burgus*, 1305; *Neuburgh*, 1324; *Newborough*, 1379) for them at Rhosyr twelve miles to the west. Adoption of the name into local

Welsh usage from the beginning ensured that the -**gh** (which in the English speech of the time would have been pronounced as the Welsh -**ch**) was retained as -**ch**. However, it would seem that Rhosyr (*Rosfeyr* 1318, probably 'moor of the seas' rather than 'the moor of Mary') was recognized as an alternative for some time (*Y Rosur alias Nuburch*, 1536–9).

NEWCASTLE EMLYN   CASTELLNEWYDD EMLYN
Carm

'the new castle in Emlyn'
castell 'castle', **newydd** 'new'

The new castle replaced the old castle at Cilgerran eight miles away and was described variously as *Novum Castrum de Emlyn* (*c.* 1240), *Emlyn with New Castle* (1257) and *Newcastle Emlyn* (1295). In Welsh it appears in 1541 as *Castell neuweydd in Emlyn*. Emlyn (*Emelinn*, 1130; *Emlyn*, 1257) was the name of the cantref which later became the Norman lordship and means 'around the valley' (**am**, **glyn**).

NEWPORT   CASNEWYDD-AR-WYSG
Monm
'new town', 'the new castle on the river Usk'
Middle English **port** 'town, market town', Welsh **cas** (**castell**) 'castle', **newydd** 'new', **ar** 'on'

The new borough established on the Usk appears in early documents as *Novus Burgus* (1138), *Nova Villa* (1290), *Neuborh* (1291). A little later it became *Neuporte* (1322) and *Newport on Husk* (1439); **port** was frequently used of a town or borough which had been granted market rights. In Welsh the reference was to the new 12th-century castle (*Castell Newyd ar Wysc*, 14th cent.; *Y Castell Newydd* 15th cent.), which was 'new' as opposed to the Roman fortification at Caerleon just over two miles away. In time **castell** was abbreviated to **cas** (as in Cas-gwent).

NEWPORT   TREFDRAETH   Pemb
'the town near the shore'
Middle English **port** 'town, market town', Welsh **tref** 'town',
traeth 'shore'

The early documents refer to the town (with market rights)
and borough (*Nuport*, 1282; *Newburgh*, 1296; *Novus Burgus*,
1316) which may have been described as 'new' in relation to
Fishguard over six miles away. The Welsh name Trefdraeth
(recorded in the 14th cent.) refers to the town's location on
the Pembrokeshire coast, while the local Welsh pronunciation has been Tredraeth (*Tredraith*, 1536–9) and Tydraeth
for some time.

NEW RADNOR   MAESYFED   Radn
'(at the) red bank' 'the field of Hyfaidd'
Old English **rēad** 'red', **ōra** 'bank', Welsh **maes** 'field'

The original Radnor, so-called from the reddish soil of the
slopes, was the present Old Radnor (Pencraig in Welsh from
pen 'top', **craig** 'rock'). In 1064 the new Radnor, less than
three miles away, was granted rights as the new administrative centre of the area (*Raddrenoue*, 1086; *Radenoura*,
1191; *Radnore*, 1201; *New Radenore*, 1298). In Welsh the
place was called *Maesyfed* after an unknown person Hyfaidd
(*Maeshyueid*, 14th cent.). Eventually the town became the
county town of Radnorshire, Sir Faesyfed.

NEWTOWN   Y DRENEWYDD   Mont
'the new town'
y 'the', **tref** 'town', **newydd** 'new'

The new settlement (*Newentone*, 1250; *the Newtown*, 1360)
developed around Llanfair-yng-Nghedewain ('the church of
St Mary in Cedewain') which continued as an alternative

name for several centuries (*new town of Kedewyng alias Llanvair in Kedewyng*, 1406). The Welsh form also refers to the new settlement (*Drenewyth in Kedewen*, 1394; *Drenewyth alias Llanvayr in Kedewen*, 1395; *Tre newydd yng-Hedewen*, 1612). In 1967, further development was encouraged when it was designated a 'new town'.

NIWBWRCH see NEWBOROUGH

YR ORSEDD see ROSSETT

OVERTON   OWRTYN   Denb
'the upper farm'
Old English **ōfer** 'upper, above', or **ofer** 'bank', **tūn** 'farm'

The name is first recorded as *Overtone* in 1201. It overlooks one of the many ox-bows in the river Dee and the farm could have been perceived as being 'above' the Dee or on the 'bank' of the river. In common with many other English place-names in this area Overton took on an alternative Welsh pronunciation and spelling (*Owrtun*, 13th cent.; *Awrtun*, 14th cent.; *Wrtun*, 15th cent.) including the distinctive -**tyn** (*Owrtyn*, 1550; *Ortyn*, 1566).

PEMBROKE   PENFRO   Pemb
'the end land'
pen 'end', **bro(g)** 'land'

The name given to the south-western tip of Wales (and later to the town) has been compared with other directional names like Land's End (Cornwall) and Finisterre (Spain) and Finistère (Brittany). The change from -**n**- to -**m**- in Pembroke (*Pembroch*, 1191; *Pembrok*, 1283) is common when -**n**- is followed by -**b**-. However, the forms with -**b**- and -**k**- are particularly intriguing; they are in a sense linguistic fossils because the British **brog** had become Welsh **bro** (and then **fro**) before 800 at the latest. The suggestion is that, for some reason, *Pennbro* (*c.* 1150), *Penbrocia* (1231) and *Penbrok*

(1245) preserve in written form features which had disappeared in everyday speech and that it was these written forms which gave rise to the pronunciation Pembroke.

PENARLÂG see **HAWARDEN**

PENARTH   Glam
'the top of the headland'
pen 'top', **garth** 'hill, ridge, promontary'

The distinctive headland is called Penarth Head. The compound **pen-garth** gave rise to a further word **pennarth** or **pennardd** 'promontory' (as in Penarlâg, Hawarden). However, the stress on the second syllable of Penarth (recorded in 1254) emphasizes the prominence of **garth** 'highland, height'.

PENMAEN-MAWR   Caern
'great stone headland'
penmaen 'stone headland' (**pen** 'top', **maen** 'rock'), **mawr** 'great'

The prominent headland (*Penmayne mawre*, 1473–4; *Penmaen mawr*, 1795) became the focus for much quarrying and for the associated growth of the village. The considerably lower mountain nearer Conwy came to be called Penmaenbach (*penmen byghan*, 1499; *Penmaen Bach* 1795) 'the little stone headland'.

PENRHYNDEUDRAETH   Mer
'promontory between two beaches'
penrhyn 'promontory', **dau** 'two', **traeth** 'beach, strand, shore'.

The two strands are Traeth Mawr (*Traitmaur*, 1194) and Traeth Bach (*Traitbochan*, 1191) (**mawr** 'big', **bach** 'little') where two rivers Glaslyn and Dwyryd flow on either side of Penrhyndeudraeth (*Penrindeudrait*, 1292–3; *penryn deudraith*, 1570) and into the Dwyryd estuary. The enclosure of Traeth Mawr and the building of the embankment to create the port of Porthmadog greatly altered the extent of the estuary.

PENTRAETH   Angl
'the end of the beach'
pen 'end', **traeth** 'beach'

Pentraeth (*Pentrayth*, 1254) is at the head of the narrow valley through which the river Nodwydd (**nodwydd** 'needle') flows into the sea at Traeth Coch (Red Wharf Bay). During the Middle Ages the names Betws Geraint and Llanfair Betws Geraint were associated with the area where the village is now.

PEN-Y-GROES   Caern
'at the top of the cross-road'
pen 'end, top', **y** 'the', **croes** 'cross'

Roads from Carmel, Rhyd-ddu and Pontlyfni cross the main Caernarfon–Porthmadog road at Pen-y-groes (1838).

PEN-Y-BONT AR OGWR   see   BRIDGEND

PONTARDAWE   Glam
'bridge over the (river) Tawe'
pont 'bridge', **ar** 'over, on'

The bridge is known to have been in existence in 1578, but early references are to a house (**tŷ**) (*Tir penybont ardawe*, 1583–4 where Tir presumably represents 'Tŷ'r'; *Ty pen y bont ar y Tawe*, 1675; *Ty pen y bont ar tawey*, 1706, 'the house at the bridge over the Tawe') and to the bridge (*Pontardowey*,

1707; *Pont ar Dawye*, 1760) making it difficult to decide whether the town took its name from the house or from the bridge. The river-name is also found in Abertawe (Swansea).

PONTARDDULAIS   Glam
'bridge over the (river) Dulais'
pont 'bridge', **ar** 'over, on'

The town grew up originally at one end of the bridge (*Ponte ar theleys*, 1557; *Dulais bridge*, 1578; *Penybont ar ddylays*, c. 1700 'the end of the bridge'). The river-name means 'dark water' (**du** 'black, dark', **glais** 'stream').

PONT HENRY   Carm
'Henry's bridge'
pont 'bridge'

Little is known about the identity of Henry and his link with the bridge across the Gwendraeth Fawr north-west of the present village. Pont Henry (*c.* 1627) and *Pont Hendry* (1760) are two of the earlier references.

PONTLLAN-FRAITH   Monm
'bridge by the speckled pool'
pont 'bridge', **llyn** 'pool, lake', **braith** 'speckled' (feminine form of **brith**)

The earlier forms (such as *tre penybont llynvraith*, 1492; *tre penbont*, 1502; and *Pontllynfraith*, 1713) demonstrate quite clearly that the reference was to a farm (**tre**) at the end of the bridge and that the middle element was **llyn** and not **llan**. In medieval Welsh **llyn** was feminine and remained so in south Wales, hence **fraith** (the mutated form of **braith** the feminine adjective of **brith**), to give the name of the pool or lake as

71

'Llyn Fraith', (probably 'speckled' from the sunlight cast on it). The bridge was over a pool in the river Sirhywi. The emergence (mainly from the 18th cent.) of forms with **llan** (*Pontlanfraith*, 1782) gave rise to the belief that there was a Saint Braith, whose name was perceived to be a form of Brigid.

PONTYPOOL see PONT-Y-PŴL

PONTYPRIDD   Glam
'bridge of the earthen house'
pont 'bridge', **y** 'the', **tŷ** 'house', **pridd** 'earth'

The early forms make it quite clear that it was the house with its distinctive walls of earth which gave a bridge its name as in *Pont y Tŷ Pridd*, *Pont y Pridd* (*c.* 1700), *Pont y Tŷ Pridd* (1764). It was probably the rapid pronunciation of normal speech which blended the similar-sounding second and third syllables, combined with the fact that the phrase 'the earthen bridge' made some sense. At least two bridges had been in existence for some time (*Newbridge* 1596–1600; *Pont y Tŷ Pridd & Pont Newidd*; *Pont newidd near Pont y pridd, c.* 1700), but it was William Edwards's new bridge, built between 1746 and 1757, which lost the association with the 'earthen house', as in *Pont y prîdd or the new bridge* (1781), *New Bridge or Pont yprydd* (1813). Newbridge was current for some time as the name of the town and also as the name of the Taff Vale Railway Station there, but it gradually fell into disuse because of confusion with Newbridge in Monmouthshire.

PONT-Y-PŴL (PONTYPOOL)   Monm
'bridge of the pool'
pont 'bridge', **y** 'the', English **pool**

The bridge crossed a pool (*Pont y poole*, 1614) in the river Llwyd (**llwyd** 'grey, dark'). The town itself developed near the parish church of Trefddyn or Trevethin and expanded rapidly with the growth of industry. The use of the English word **pool** (rather than the Welsh **pwll**) is interesting, as is its adoption of a Welsh spelling **pŵl**.

PORTHAETHWY see MENAI BRIDGE

PORTH-CAWL   Glam
'sea-kale harbour'
porth 'harbour', **cawl** 'sea-kale'

Cawl is used of 'cabbage' and of the broth or soup made of vegetables. The sea-kale must have grown abundantly or even been collected here (*Portcall*, 1632; *Pwll Cawl o(r) Porth Cawl*, 1825 where **pwll** means 'pool'). The current anglicized pronunciation is reflected in the 1632 spelling, influenced possibly by the fact that **cawl** is the same word as appears in 'cauli(flower)' and 'cole(-slaw)'*;* indeed sea-kale was frequently written and pronounced 'sea-cole'.

PORTHMADOG   Caern
'port of Madocks'
English **port** 'port', Welsh **porth** 'harbour, port'

Between 1800 and his death in 1828 William Alexander Madocks (the Member of Parliament for Boston, Lincoln-shire) was responsible for enclosing a large area of the marsh and shore called Traeth Mawr (*Trait mawr*, 1194 'the great strand'). He developed the village of Tremadoc (*Tre-madoc*, 1810, **tre** 'large village, town'), constructed an embankment (the Cob), and built a harbour (*Portmadoc*, 1838) to export slate from the Blaenau Ffestiniog quarries. The two names which commemorate Madocks, Tremadoc and Portmadoc, later adopted Welsh versions as Tremadog and Porthmadog probably influenced by the Welsh personal name Madog.

PORT TALBOT   Glam

In 1836 new docks were built at Aberafan Harbour to export
iron and coal. The landowners were the Talbot family,
originally from Wiltshire, who had inherited Margam Abbey
in the previous century.

PRESTATYN   Flints
'farm of the priests'
Old English **prēosta** 'of the priests', **tūn** 'farm'

Farms supporting, or run by, priests were fairly common,
and in England the place-names usually develop to Preston.
In Flintshire, however, the name, which is found quite early
(*Prestetone*, 1086), took on a distinctively Welsh character.
The middle syllable, instead of being swallowed (as in
Preston), survived by adopting the regular Welsh stress on
the penultimate syllable of a word (*Prestatton*, 1301). Then
the last syllable, instead of becoming **-ton,** followed the Welsh
sound system to become **-tyn** (*Prestatyn*, 1536) as in several -
ton names in Flintshire (such as Mostyn, Mertyn and
Golftyn).

PRESTEIGNE   LLANANDRAS   Radn
'household of the priests' 'the church of St Andreas'
Old English **prēosta** 'of the priests', **hæmed** 'household',
Welsh **llan** 'church'

The location, identity and significance of the community of
priests are not known despite the name being well documented (*Prestehemed*, 1137–39; *Prestene* 1548). The church is
dedicated to Andreas (Andrew) (*Llanandras*, 1286).

PWLLHELI Caern
'brine pool'
pwll 'pool', **heli** 'brine, saltwater'

It is not certain whether this was a pool which was replenished by the tide, or the almost entirely enclosed natural inlet which forms the harbour (*Pwllhely* 1292–3).

QUEENSFERRY Flints

There were several ferries across the river Dee before and after it was canalized in 1737. One of them was the Lower Ferry (1726), with the Higher Ferry being at Saltney. Eventually, the Lower Ferry's name was changed to the Lower King's Ferry or simply King's Ferry (1828) in honour of George IV. At the coronation of Queen Victoria in 1837 the name was further changed to Queensferry.

RADUR Glam
'oratory'
Latin **oratorium** 'oratory'

An oratory is a small chapel, usually for private worship. The early forms (*Radur*, 1254; *Rador*, 1291; *Aradur*, 13th cent.) have caused some to suggest that Radur was a personal name in this instance. Certainly the form Aradur, which occurs several times, could lead to the pronunciation Y Radur (as if it were **y** 'the'). It is frequently misspelt Radyr.

RAGLAN RHAGLAN Monm
'rampart'
rhag 'before, against', **glan** 'bank'

In the 11th century, there was a motte-and-bailey castle

(*Raghelan*, 1254) where the remains of the 15th-century castle now stand.

RHAEADR (GWY) (RHAYADER) Radn
'waterfall' (on the river Gwy)
rhaeadr 'waterfall'

The impact of the spectacular waterfall was diminished by the road bridge built in 1780. From the earliest record (*Raidergoe*, 1191) the river-name Gwy (Wye) has frequently been attached to the name of the waterfall and the town (as in *Rayadyr Gwy*, 14th cent.; *Raiadergwy*, 1543). The anglicized spelling has little justification today.

RHISGA (RISCA) Monm
'bark'
rhisgau possible plural of **rhisg** 'bark'

It has been tentatively suggested that the place's name (*Risca*, 1330) could be attributed to a house built of logs with the bark still on them or of bark used as shingles on the walls. However, the hypothetical **rhisgau** as a plural of **rhisg** or **rhisgl** is not found independently of this place-name.

RHIWABON RUABON Denb
'hill of Mabon'
rhiw 'hill'

The identity of Mabon is unknown but his name did remain a distinct feature of the place-name for some time (*Rywnabon*, 1291 where the -*n*- probably represents -*v*-; *Rhiwvabon*, 1394; *Rhiw vabon*, 1566). There was an alternative form in use from fairly early on (*Riwabon*, 1397; *Ruabon*, 1461) and this was the form which survived.

RHONDDA   Glam
'noisy (river)'
rhoddni 'noisy, babbling'

The river-name is used of two rivers, the Rhondda Fawr
(**mawr** 'great') and Rhondda Fach (or Fechan) (**bach** 'little'),
which in earlier records appear as *Rotheni mawr* (1203),
Rodeney vawr (1536–9), *Rhondda fawr* (1833), and as *Roth-
eney vehan* (1536–39), *Ronthey vechan* (1666), *Rhonddafechan*
(1799). The river-name gave rise to the name of the valley
(**glyn**) as Glyn Rhoddni (*Glenrotheny*, 1268). In time, Rhoddni and the variant Rhoddne became Rhonddi and Rhondda,
with the latter surviving as the dialect form Rhondda. The
practice of referring to The Rhondda can probably be
ascribed to the association with the rivers or with Glyn
Rhondda.

RHOSLLANNERCHRUGOG   Denb
'moor of the heather glade'
rhos 'heath, moor', **llannerch** 'cleaning, glade', **grugog** 'of
heather' (**grug**)

The length of the name has always presented a challenge (as
is demonstrated by *Rose lane aghregog*, 1544–5) and has
frequently led to the use of Rhos as a convenient abbreviation (*Rowse*, 1698), as is the custom now.

RHOS-ON-SEA   LLANDRILLO-YN-RHOS   Denb
'the moor by the sea', the church of (St) Trillo in Rhos'
rhos 'moor', **llan** 'church', **yn** 'in, on'

Rhos was the medieval administrative cantref and the name
was added to the older Llandrillo (1538) as Llandrillo-yn-
Rhos (*Llandrillo in Rhose*, 1691). The 'English' name is
recent, having been coined in the 19th century to highlight

the area's attraction (as with nearby Colwyn Bay). By now, a perceived distinction exists between the village of Llandrillo-yn-Rhos and the resort of Rhos-on-Sea.

RHOSTRYFAN Caern
'moor of (the hill called Moel) Tryfan'
rhos 'moor'

The hill near Rhostryfan (*Rhos Tryfan*, 1827) is Moel Tryfan, from **moel** 'bare (hill)' and **tryfan** 'the distinctive summit, sharp peak' (from **try** 'exceptional' and **ban** 'summit'). Early records refer to the hill as Moel Dryfan and Y Foel Dryfan.

RHOSTYLLEN Denb
'the moor on a ledge'
rhos 'moor', **astell, astyllen** 'ledge of rock'

An early form is *Rhos Stellan* (1546). The usual meaning of **astell** or **astyllen** was 'plank, board', but here it is used figuratively of a ledge of rock, above the meadows beside the river Clywedog. Another variant, **ystyllen** 'plank, lath', seems to have influenced the spelling of *Rhôs ystyllen* (*c.* 1700).

RHUDDLAN Flints
'red bank'
rhudd 'red', **glan** 'bank'

The banks of the river Clwyd are distinctively red at this point. The early records (*Roelend*, 1086; *Ruthelan*, 1191) occur in the context of English and Norman-French settlements with the first reference also showing the influence of the English **land** (as does *Ruthland*, 1582). The 14th-century form *Rudlan* reflects an anglicized pronunciation which is still heard today.

RHUTHUN (RUTHIN)   Denb
'red fort'
rhudd 'red', **din** 'fort'

There is still evidence of the red sandstone in the ruins of the
13th-century castle (*Ruthun*, 1253), which in 1545–53 was
referred to as *Y Castell Coch yng gwernfor* (**y** 'the', **castell**
'castle', **coch** 'red', **yn** 'in'); Gwernfor (**gwern** 'marsh', **fawr**
'great') was the extensive marsh.

RHYDAMAN see AMMANFORD

RHYL   Flints
'the hill'
yr 'the', Middle English **hull** 'hill'

The early forms show this to be the Middle English word for
hill (*Hull*, 1302) to which has been added the Welsh **yr** 'the'
(as in *Ryhull*, 1301; *Yrhill*, 1578; *Rhyll*, 1660; *Rhil*, 1706). The
exact significance of the hill is more problematic since there is
no feature currently worthy of the name. In such a flat
terrain, however, the slightest eminence could have been
given the title of 'hill'. Other suggestions are that the hill was
a mound thrown up by the extraction of salt from salt-pools
(as in Lincolnshire) or that **hill** is a variant of the dialect **hyle**,
hoyle 'sand-bank' (as in Hoylake in the Wirral). The inability
to identify the hill probably explains why the spelling is not
'Rhill'.

RHYMNI (RHYMNEY)   Monm
'the auger river'
rhwmp 'auger, borer', **ni** (adjectival ending)

The river Rhymni rises south of Mynydd Llangynidr and
flows through the present town and on through the Rhymney
Valley to enter the sea east of Cardiff. For its entire length it

was the boundary between Glamorgan and Monmouthshire. Several river-names describe the action of boring or cutting through land. Some versions of this river-name retained the **-p-** for some time (*Rempny*, 1296; *Rumpny*, 1681) while others lost it very early on (*Remni*, 1101–20; *Rymney*, 1541). The industrial town developed around the various ironworks established initially at Blaenrhymni in 1801 before eventually forming The Rhymney Ironwork Company in 1836. The community for which the ironworks provided a livelihood appears to have taken its name from the ironworks rather than from the river. The river has also given its name to another, much older, Rhymni near Cardiff where the manor and castle were situated, as well as the church (*ecclesia de Rempney*, 1291). However, the **llan** of Llanrhymni (*Llan-rumney*, 1630) is misleading; it was originally 'Glanrhymney', on the bank (**glan**) of the Rhymni.

RISCA see **RHISGA**

ROSSETT   YR ORSEDD   Denb
'the hill'
yr 'the', **gorsedd** 'hill'

Rossett seems to have replaced one of the place-names of the Domesday Book (1086), that of *Radenoure*, which means 'at the red hill' (Old English **readan** 'red', **ōra** 'bank'). By 1391 the edge of the sandstone and gravel escarpment south of Marford Hill was called *yr allt goch* (**gallt** 'hill', **coch** 'red'). The actual Orsedd Goch (*le Orseth Goch*, 1473; *yr orsedd goch*, 1530) may have been more specifically the part of the hill behind the Trevor Arms at Marford on which the motte of Roft Castle was built inside an Iron Age fort. It was the form Yr Orsedd which became Rhosedd (*Rhossedh*, c. 1700) and was then anglicized to Rossett (*Rossett Goch*, 1554), influenced by the association of 'red hill' with 'russett'. Rossett is just under a mile from the motte, but the naming must have been prompted by the dominant feature of Yr

Orsedd as seen from the water-meadows at Rossett. Several examples of Gorsedd and Yr Orsedd used of a hill are to be found in Wales, some associated with a tumulus. A number are in Flintshire and Denbighshire, including Bryn Rossett north of Hanmer where there is a tumulus. It was much later that **gorsedd** came to be used of a throne, and of the eisteddfodic gathering of bards.

RUABON see **RHIWABON**

RUTHIN see **RHUTHUN**

ST ASAPH   LLANELWY   Denb
'(church of) St Asaph' 'the church on the (river) Elwy'
llan 'church'

The cathedral is dedicated to the 6th-century bishop and saint Asaph or Asaff (*Ecclesia Cathedralis de Sancto Asaph*, 1291). The Welsh name refers to the location of the cathedral beside the river Elwy (*Lanhelewey*, 1345; *Lanelwy*, 1365).

ST CLEARS   SANCLÊR   Carm
'(church of) St Clear'

The earliest references are *Ecclesia de Sancto Claro* (1291) and *Seint Cler* (1331). The 9th-century saint is also commemorated in St Cleer in Cornwall (*Seintcler*, 1230) and in St Clair in Normandy.

ST DAVIDS   TYDDEWI   Pemb
'(church of) St David' 'house of Dewi (Sant)'
tŷ 'house'

The village takes its name from the cathedral dedicated to St David or Dewi Sant. In the Welsh name **tŷ** is used in the biblical sense of 'house (of the Lord)' (*Tŷ Dewi* 1586). The Latin (and biblical) David(us) became Dewydd in Welsh, and hence the later personal name Dewi (while the alternative Welsh personal name Dafydd is a direct adaptation of David).

SANCLÊR see ST CLEARS

SHOTTON   Flint
'farm on a hill'
Old English **scēot** 'hill', **tūn** 'farm'

The original farm (*Schotton*, 1283–5) was in what is now called Higher Shotton on the hill above Lower Shotton beside the river Dee. Industrial expansion, particularly the John Summers or Shotton Steelworks, has been within Lower Shotton and on both banks of the Dee, so that today the name Shotton is linked more readily with these urban developments.

SWANSEA ABERTAWE   Glam
'island of Sveinn' 'mouth of the (river) Tawe'
Old Norse **ey** 'island', Welsh **aber** 'river-mouth, estuary'

Swansea is further evidence of the Scandinavian presence along the south Wales coast. The identity of the Viking Sveinn is not known, but he may be associated here with an island in the estuary referred to as *Iselond* in 1432, and as *The Island* in 1641. Over the centuries the spelling and meaning of the last syllable have been influenced by **sea**. The river Tawe (*Tauuy, c.* 1150) flows into the sea here (*Aper Tyui, c.* 1150; *Abertawi*, 12th cent.).

TALACHARN see LAUGHARNE

TALGARTH   Brec
'end of the ridge'
tâl 'end', **garth** 'ridge, hillside, wooded slope'

Talgarth (1100) is at the edge of the extensive hill country
north-west of the Black Mountain.

TAL-Y-BONT   Card
'bridge-end'
tâl 'the end of', **pont** 'bridge'

The village of Tal-y-bont (*Talebont*, 1301; *Talybont*, 1654) is
at the northern end of the bridge over the river Leri.

TAL-Y-SARN   Caern
'the end of the causeway'
tâl 'end', **y** 'the', **sarn** 'causeway'

The causeway carried the route from Rhyd-ddu and Llyn
Nantlle to Tal-y-sarn (*Talysarn*, 1795) across the wetlands on
either side of the slow-moving river Llyfni (**llyfn** 'smooth').

TENBY see **DINBYCH-Y-PYSGOD**

TONYPANDY   Glam
'grassland of the fulling mill'
ton 'grassland, lay-land', **y** 'the', **pandy** 'fulling-mill'

Grassland left unploughed for some time was referred to as
ton, a word which seems to be limited to Gwent, parts of
south Breconshire and particularly Glamorgan (as in Ton-
teg, Tonyrefail, Tonpentre, Ton-du and Tongwynlais). The
fulling-mill beside the Rhondda (Fawr) was in existence from
the 18th century until early this century.

TRALLWNG see **WELSHPOOL**

TRAWSFYNYDD   Mer
'across the mountain'
traws 'across', **mynydd** 'mountain'

The village is central to several mountain routes, the more
obvious today being those to Bala, Ffestiniog and Dolgellau.
The extensive Roman settlement at Tomen-y-mur near the
roadside a few miles to the north points to a long-established
strategic route. An early form is *Trausvenith* (1292–3), but it
also appears to have been called Trawsbryn or Trawsybryn
(**bryn** 'hill') at one stage (*Trausbrin o[r] Trausvenithe*, 1562;
Trawsvynith o[r] Trawsybryn, 1636).

TREARDDUR   Angl
'farm of Iarddur'
tre 'farm'

Iarddur was a notable medieval figure, and his farm was one
of the largest in north-west Anglesey. The advent of the
railway and tourism ensured the rapid growth of the hamlet,
and its seaside location was further publicized by its
designation as Trearddur Bay. Early forms are *Tre Iarthur*
(1609) and *Treyarddur* (1691).

TREDEGAR   Monm
'farm of Tegyr'
tre 'farm'

The Tredegar family took its name from the family home at
Tredegar or Tredegyr near Newport (Monmouthshire)
(*Tredegyr*, 1550; *Tredeger*, 1551; *Tredegar*, 1632). In 1800 the
Tredegar Iron Works was established on land belonging to
the family fifteen miles to the north-west at the top of the
Sirhywi valley. It was this ironworks which gave its name to
the community which developed nearby and which depended

on the works for a living. In 1860 Thomas Powell opened New Tredegar Colliery in the adjacent valley and the surrounding hamlets came to be called New Tredegar.

TREFNANT   Denb
'the hamlet on the brook'
tref 'farm, hamlet', **nant** 'brook'

The hamlet developed near Nant Padrig at the junction of roads from Tremeirchion, Henllan, St Asaph and Denbigh. An early form is *Trevenant* (1661–2), which suggests it was originally 'Tref-y-Nant' (**y** 'the'). Trefnant is recorded in 1839, but it was almost certainly in use before that.

TREFFYNNON see HOLYWELL

TREFRIW   Caern
'farm of the hill'
tref 'farm', **rhiw** 'hill'

The original farm (*Treffruu*, 1254) was near a very steep hill now within the village.

TREFYCLO see KNIGHTON

TREGARON   Card
'hamlet on the (river) Caron'
tre 'farm, hamlet'

Early forms are *tre garon* (1566) and *Caron alias Tre Garon* (1763). The church is dedicated to St Caron and the parish was called Caron (*Karaun*, 1284). The river also took the name Caron, rising in Blaencaron (**blaen** 'headwater') and flowing past Tregaron on to the river Teifi.

TREGŴYR see GOWERTON

TREORCI   Glam
'village on the (stream) Orci'
tre 'village'

The town stands on a tributary of Rhondda (Fawr) called
Orci or Gorci, the exact significance of which is unknown. To
the north of the town is Fforchorci (**fforch** 'fork of a river')
and a farm Aberorci. 'English' usage tends to favour Tre-
orchy, but the **-ch-** is late and has little justification.

TYDDEWI see **ST DAVIDS**

TYWYN   Mer
'sea-shore'
tywyn 'sandy shore, sand-dune'

The Meirionethshire Tywyn was first recorded as *Thewyn*
(1254) and *Tewyn* (1291) and later as *Towyn Meronnygh*
(1461). There are two other examples of Tywyn, one near
Cardigan and another near Abergele (which frequently
appears in the anglicized form Towyn).

USK   BRYNBUGA   Monm
'(town on the river) Usk' 'the hill of Buga'
bryn 'hill'

The Romans adopted the British river-name as the name of
their fort at Isca (Caerleon) and it appears later as *Uscha*
(1100), *Uisc* (1150) and *Wysc* (13th cent.), the modern Welsh
form being Wysg. The meaning of Usk and Wysg is probably
'abounding in fish'. The Welsh name Brynbuga is recorded in
1450–1500 but the identity of Buga is lost.

VALLEY   (Y FALI)   Angl

The name emerged as a consequence of the building of the

Cob or Stanley Embankment from mainland Anglesey to Holy Island and the associated Telford post-road to Holyhead in 1822–3. The origin is the valley-like cutting from which rubble was extracted for the Embankment. In 1825 there is a reference to '*the Embankment or Valley*', and in the same year a nearby public house is referred to as Valley. Soon the hamlet (inhabited mainly by Irish labourers) was called Valley (and occasionally Pentre Gwyddelod 'village of the Irish'). Later, the station, rail-head and cross-roads a little further away came to be called Valley, and the original hamlet became Hen Valley 'old Valley'. The translation into Welsh as Dyffryn has little justification since local usage has long adopted Y Fali 'the Valley', a name which reinforces the allusion to the original valley.

Y WAUN see CHIRK

WELSHPOOL   Y TRALLWNG   Mont
'the Welsh pool' 'the very wet quagmire'
English **pool**, Welsh **y** 'the', **tra** 'very', **llwng** 'slough, swamp, pool'

The early forms simply refer to the Pool (*Pola* 1253; *La Pole*, 1278; *Poole*, 1411) formed where the Lledin brook flows into the river Severn. The location very close to the border caused the addition of a distinguishing 'Welsh' (*Walshe Pole*, 1477) (as in English Frankton and Welsh Frankton), although in this instance no 'Englishpool' has been identified. The Welsh name Y Trallwng appears as *Trallwg Llywelyn* 'the pool of Llywelyn' in the 14th century and as *y trallwn* in 1566. The variant **trallwm** for **trallwng** is frequently used as Trallwm.

WHITLAND   HEN-DŶ-GWYN AR DAF   Carm
'the white glade' 'the old white house (on the river Taf)'
Old English **hwīt** 'white', Old French **launde** 'glade', Welsh
hen 'old', **tŷ** 'house', **gwyn** 'white', **ar** 'on'

The original name was Tŷ Gwyn 'the white house' probably
after an earlier monastery (*ty gwyn ar daf*, 13th cent.; *y ty
gwyn*, 14th cent.). Some Latin ecclesiastical documents translated the name as *Alba Domus* (1191), while other Latin and
Norman-French documents referred to the site as *Alba Landa*
(1214), *Blaunchelande* (1318), *Blancalanda* (1329) and in
English as Whitland (recorded in 1309) and *Whiteland*
(1352). In time, the house became 'the old house' hence the
addition of **hen** as in *Hendygwyn* (1561). The addition 'on the
Taf' dates from the 13th century (*ty gwyn ar daf*).

WREXHAM   (WRECSAM)   Denb
'the water-meadow of Wryhtel'
Old English **hamm** 'water-meadow, pasture'

The undulating rivers Gwenfro and Clywedog provided the
water-meadows which were associated with an unidentified
Wryhtel (*Wristlesham*, 1161; *Wrexham*, 1186). There were
several Welsh versions of the name (*Gwregsam*, 1291;
Gwreksam, c. 1566) but only Wrecsam is now generally
recognized.

YR WYDDGRUG see **MOLD**

YSTALYFERA   Glam
'the meadow at the end of the short share-land'
ynys 'meadow in wet land or beside a river', **tâl** 'end', **y** 'the',
possibly **berran** 'short share-land'

Early forms (*Ynys Tal y Veran*, 1582; *Tir Ynystalverran*,
1604) indicate a meadow surrounded by wetter ground or
beside a river (Tawe, in this instance) which was at the end of

a **berran**. This is a hypothetical word which is not evidenced independently of this place-name; it is made up of **ber** 'short' and **rhan** 'part, share' and might have indicated land shared by two or more tenants. Later forms indicate the gradual loss of **ynys** as a recognizable word (*Staleyfera*, 1729; *Ystal-y-fera*, 1831). In 1839 an ironworks was built here which gave currency to the form used ever since.

YSTRADGYNLAIS Brec
'the vale of Cynlais'
ystrad 'valley-floor'

Ystrad appears in a number of place-names, signifying an open valley-bottom and associated meadows. (The word **ystrad** is related to **strath** in Scottish place-names and corresponds to Latin **strata**, as in Ystrad Fflur, Strata Florida.) The identity of Cynlais is unknown. Early forms of Ystradgynlais are *Stradgenles* (1372) and *Estradgynles* (1493).

YSTRADMYNACH Glam
'vale of the monk'
ystrad 'valley-floor', **mynach** 'monk'

Early forms are *Ystrad manach* (1635, where **manach** is a dialectical variant of **mynach**) and *Ystrad y Mynach* (1833, **y** 'the'). However, there is no evidence of a monastic settlement here in the Rhymni Valley. Mynach may have been the (lost) name of a tributary of the Rhymni but the reason for such a name is not known. (For a discussion of **ystrad** see the entry for Ystradgynlais.)

Further Reading

In English, the standard authoritative dictionary of place-names which includes Wales is M. Gelling, W. F. H. Nicolaisen, M. Richards, *The Names of Towns and Cities in Britain* (Batsford 1970, 1986).

Other general reference books (in Welsh or English):

J. Field, *Place-Names in Great Britain and Ireland* (David & Charles, 1980).

A. Lias, *A Guide to Welsh Place-Names* (Carreg Gwalch, 1994).

A. Room, *Dictionary of Place-Names in the British Isles* (Bloomsbury, 1988).

I. Williams, *Enwau Lleoedd* (Gwasg y Brython, 1945, 1969).

Regional reference books (in Welsh or English):

B. G. Charles, *The Place-Names of Pembrokeshire* (National Library of Wales, 1992), 2 volumes.

E. Davies, *Flintshire Place-Names* (University of Wales, 1959).

D. John, *Cynon Valley Place-names* (Carreg Gwalch, 1998).

G. T. Jones, T. Roberts, *Place-names of Anglesey* (Isle of Anglesey County Council, 1996), (bilingual).

J. Lloyd-Jones, *Enwau Lleoedd Sir Gaernarfon* (University of Wales, 1928).

R. Morgan, G. G. Evans, *Enwau Lleoedd Buallt a Maesyfed* (Carreg Gwalch, 1993).

H. W. Owen, *The Place-Names of East Flintshire* (University of Wales, 1994).

H. W. Owen, *Enwau Lleoedd* (Canolfan Astudiaethau Addysg, 1990).

H. W. Owen, *Enwau Lleoedd Bro Dyfrdwy ac Alun* (Carreg Gwalch, 1991), (also available in English).

G. O. Pierce, *The Place-Names of Dinas Powys Hundred* (University of Wales, 1968).

Other books in Welsh:

B. L. Jones, *Enwau* (Carreg Gwalch, 1991).

B. L. Jones, *Yn Ei Elfen* (Carreg Gwalch, 1992).

G. O. Pierce, T. Roberts, H. W. Owen, *Ar Draws Gwlad* (Carreg Gwalch, 1997).

M. Richards (ed. B. L. Jones), *Enwau Tir a Gwlad* (Gwasg Gwynedd, 1998).

Most county or local history series in Wales include detailed articles in journals or in occasional publications.

A bibliography of place-name publications in Wales is contained in J. Spittal, J. Field, *A Reader's Guide to the Place-names of the United Kingdom* (Paul Watkins, 1990).

Index

Other place-names, hills, rivers, and persons referred to in the discussion of the major names.

Brefi	LLANDDEWI BREFI
Britannia Bridge	LLANFAIR PWLLGWYNGYLL
Brithdir	BARGOED
Brychdyn	BROUGHTON
Brycheiniog	BRECON
Bryn Rossett	ROSSETT
Buellt	BUILTH
Burry Holms	BURRY PORT
Caer Ddygant	DEGANNWY
Caereinion	LLANFAIR CAEREINION
Caerhun	CONWY
Calcott	CALDICOT
Canovium	CONWY
Caron	TREGARON
Carn Fadrun	ABER-SOCH
Castell Baldwin	MONTGOMERY
Castell Dolbadarn	LLANBERIS
Castle Hill	MONTGOMERY
Castrum Leonis	HOLT
Cefn Pennar	MOUNTAIN ASH
Cefn-y-bedd	CAERGWRLE
Ceidio	BAGLAN, LLANGEITHO
Ceidio(g)	LLANGEITHO
Ceredigion	CARDIGAN
Cilgerran	NEWCASTLE EMLYN
Claudagh	CLYDACH
Clawdd Offa	KNIGHTON
Cleddau	MILFORD HAVEN, ABERGELE, HAVERFORDWEST
Cloydagh	CLYDACH
Clwyd	RHUDDLAN
Clyde	CLYDACH
Clywedog	CLYDACH, WREXHAM
Coalbrookvale	NANT-Y-GLO
Cob	PORTHMADOG, VALLEY
Coed y Ddôl	LLANBERIS
Coran	LAUGHARNE

Corley	CAERGWRLE
Crickadarn	CRUCYWEL
Crickheath	CRUCYWEL
Crick	CRUCYWEL
Cross Inn	AMMANFORD
Crucadarn	CRUCYWEL
Cwm Afon	ABERSYCHAN
Cwm Aman	BRYNAMAN
Cwm Bargoed	BARGOED
Cwm Baw	BRYMBO
Cwm Berwyn	LLANDDEWI BREFI
Cwm Clydach	CLYDACH
Cwmllwchwr	LOUGHOR
Cwmpennar	MOUNTAIN ASH
Cynon	ABERDÂR, MOUNTAIN ASH
Dâr	ABERDÂR
Daron	ABERDARON
Decantae	DEGANNWY
Dee	BALA, CEFN-MAWR, CONNAH'S QUAY, FLINT, HAWARDEN, HOLT, OVERTON, QUEENSFERRY, SHOTTON
Desert	DISERTH
Dinorwig	DEINIOLEN, Y FELINHELI
Disert	DISERTH
Diwlas	DOWLAIS
Du	DOLGARROG
Dulais	DOWLAIS, LLANDDULAS
Dulas	LLANDDULAS
Dulyn	DOLGARROG
Dwyryd	PENRHYNDEUDRAETH
Dyffryn	VALLEY
Dyffryn Ceiriog	LLANSANFFRAID GLAN CONWY
Dyfi	MACHYNLLETH, ABERDOVEY
Dygant	DEGANNWY

Dysart	DISERTH
Dywlais	DOWLAIS
Dywlas	DOWLAIS
Ebeneser	DEINIOLEN
Ebwy	EBBW VALE
Ebwy Fach	ABERTYLERI
Eithinog	CLYNNOG
Elwy	ST ASAPH
Emlyn	NEWCASTLE EMLYN
English Frankton	WELSHPOOL
Esgair Llethr	LLANDDEWI BREFI
Ewyas	LLANDDEWI NANT HODDNI
Farndon	HOLT
Fforchorci	TREORCI
Ffynnongroyw	GRONANT
Finistère	PEMBROKE
Finisterre	PEMBROKE
Foel Dryfan	RHOSTRYFAN
Foel Gurig	LLANGURIG
Gafenni	ABERGAFENNI
Gele	ABERGELE
Gest	BORTH-Y-GEST
Glan Conwy	LLANSANFFRAID GLAN CONWY
Glanaman	BRYNAMAN
Glaslyn	PENRHYNDEUDRAETH
Glyn Hoddnant	LLANDDEWI NANT HODDNI
Glyn Rhoddni	RHONDDA
Glynceiriog	LLANSANFFRAID GLAN CONWY
Golftyn	BROUGHTON, PRESTATYN
Gorsedd	ROSSETT
Gower (Road)	GOWERTON
Gwaun	FISHGUARD
Gwaun Caegurwen	CLYDACH
Gwaun-helygen	BRYN-MAWR
Gwenfro	WREXHAM

Gwent	BLAENAU, CAER-WENT, CHEPSTOW
Gwernfor	RHUTHUN
Gwy	RHAEADR
Gwydderig	LLANYMDDYFRI
Gwynlais	DOWLAIS
Gŵyr	GOWERTON
Gwytherin	BAGLAN
Hay Bluff	LLANDDEWI NANT HODDNI
Hen Domen	MONTGOMERY
Hen Valley	VALLEY
Henrhyd Falls	ABER-CRAF
Hereford	HAVERFORDWEST
Higher Ferry	QUEENSFERRY
Higher Shotton	SHOTTON
Hoddnant	ABER-PORTH, LLANDDEWI NANT HODDNI
Hoddni	ABER-PORTH, BRECON, LLANDDEWI NANT HODDNI
Holy Island	HOLYHEAD, VALLEY
Honddu	BRECON, LLANDDEWI NANT HODDNI
Hwch	ABER-SOCH
Ilston	LLANILLTUD FAWR
Isca	USK
Isca Legionis	CAERLEON
King's Ferry	QUEENSFERRY
Lacharn	LAUGHARNE
Land's End	PEMBROKE
Leinster	ABER-SOCH
Leri	TAL-Y-BONT
Llan Sain Siôr	LLANSANFFRAID GLAN CONWY
Llanarmon Dyffryn Ceiriog	LLANSANFFRAID GLYNCEIRIOG
Llandaf(f)	CARDIFF
Llanddeiniolen	DEINIOLEN

Llanddwy	LLANDRINDOD
Llandysilio	LLANFAIR PWLLGWYNGYLL
Llandysiliogogo	LLANFAIR PWLLGWYNGYLL
Llan-faes	NEWBOROUGH
Llanfaglan	BAGLAN
Llanfair Betws Geraint	PENTRAETH
Llanfair-yng-Nghedewain	NEWTOWN
Llanfihangel Iorath	LLANFIHANGEL-AR-ARTH
Llanfihangel-yn-Rug	LLANRUG
Llangeinwen	CLYNNOG
Llangyngar	LLANGEFNI
Llanilltud Fach	LLANILLTUD FAWR
Llanilltud Faerdref	LLANILLTUD FAWR
Llanilltud Gŵyr	LLANILLTUD FAWR
Llanilltud Nedd	LLANILLTUD FAWR
Llanilltud-iuxta-Neath	LLANILLTUD FAWR
Llantwit Fardre	LLANILLTUD FAWR
Lledin	WELSHPOOL
Llwyd	ABERSYCHAN, CWM-BRÂN, PONT-Y-PŴL
Llwyni	MAES-TEG
Llyfni	LLANLLYFNI, TAL-Y-SARN
Llyn Nantlle	LLANLLYFNI, TAL-Y-SARN
Llyn Padarn	LLANBERIS
Llyn Peris	LLANBERIS
Llyn Tegid	BALA
Llys y Llewod	HOLT
Lower (King's) Ferry	QUEENSFERRY
Lower Shotton	SHOTTON
Lyons	HOLT
Maglona	MACHYNLLETH
Maldwyn	MONTGOMERY
Marford Hill	ROSSETT
Margam	PORT TALBOT
Maridunum	CARMARTHEN
Mawdd	BARMOUTH
Mawddach	BARMOUTH

Mawddwy	BARMOUTH
Mellte	GLYN-NEATH
Mertyn	PRESTATYN
Minera	COED-POETH
Moel Arthur	MOELFRE
Moel Dywyll	MOELFRE
Moel Fama	MOELFRE
Moel Hiraddug	DISERTH
Moel Siabod	MOELFRE
Moel Tryfan	RHOSTRYFAN
Moel y Gest	BORTH-Y-GEST
Moel y Parc	MOELFRE
Monnow	LLANDDEWI NANT HODDNI, MONMOUTH
Morlais	DOWLAIS
Mostyn	BROUGHTON, PRESTATYN
Mynwy	MONMOUTH
Mynydd Blaenafan	CWMAFAN
Mynydd Llangynidr	RHYMNI
Mynydd Twr	HOLYHEAD
Mynydd y Betws	CLYDACH
Mynydd y Fochriw	BARGOED
Mynydd y Gwair	CLYDACH
Nant Brân	CWM-BRÂN
Nant Padrig	TREFNANT
Nant Peris	LLANBERIS
Nanthoddni	LLANDDEWI NANT HODDNI
Nant-llech Bellaf	ABER-CRAF
Nash	NARBERTH
Nedd	NEATH
Nevern	CRYMYCH
New Tredegar	TREDEGAR
Newbridge	PONTYPRIDD
Nidd	NEATH
Nidum	NEATH
Nodwydd	ABERDAUGLEDDAU, PENTRAETH

Nova Villa	NEWPORT
Novum Castrum	NEWCASTLE EMLYN
Novus Burgus	NEWBOROUGH, NEWPORT
Oakdale	BARGOED
Offa's Dyke	KNIGHTON
Ogmore	BRIDGEND
Ogwen	ABER-SOCH
Old Radnor	NEW RADNOR
Orsedd Goch	ROSSETT
Pembre Burrows	BURRY PORT
Pencraig	NEW RADNOR
Pen-bre	MOELFRE
Penmaen-bach	PENMAEN-MAWR
Pennar	MOUNTAIN ASH
Pentre Broughton	BROUGHTON
Pentre Gwyddelod	VALLEY
Pen-y-cae	EBBW VALE
Penycoed	BARGOED
Pen y Pass	LLANBERIS
Pen-y-waun	HIRWAUN
Pont y Borth	MENAI BRIDGE
Pontlyfni	LLANLLYFNI
Pool	WELSHPOOL
Port Dinorwig	Y FELINHELI
Porth Amlwch	AMLWCH
Porth-llwyd	DOLGARROG
Porth Wygyr	CEMAES
Preston	PRESTATYN
Pwllgwyngyll	LLANFAIR PWLLGWYNGYLL
Pyrddin	GLYN-NEATH
Radenoure	ROSSETT
Radnorshire	NEW RADNOR
Red Wharf Bay	PENTRAETH
Rheidol	ABERYSTWYTH
Rhodogeidio	LLANGEITHO
Rhos	RHOSLLANNERCHRUGOG, RHOS-ON-SEA

Rhosaman	BRYNAMAN
Rhos-y-bol	BORTH-Y-GEST
Rhosymedre	CEFN-MAWR
Rhosyr	NEWBOROUGH
Rhyd-ddu	TAL-Y-SARN
Roft Castle	ROSSETT
Rug	LLANRUG
Sain Ffagan	LLANSANFFRAID GLAN CONWY
Sain Ffrêd	LLANSANFFRAID GLAN CONWY
Sain Tathan	LLANSANFFRAID GLAN CONWY
Saint	CAERNARFON
Saint-y-brid	LLANSANFFRAID GLAN CONWY
Segontium	CAERNARFON
Seion	CAERNARFON
Senghennydd	CAERFFILI
Sir Drefaldwyn	MONTGOMERY
Sir Faesyfed	NEW RADNOR
Sirhywi	PONTLLAN-FRAITH
Sketty	CILGETI
Soch	ABER-SOCH
St Athan	LLANSANFFRAID GLAN CONWY
St Brides Major	LLANSANFFRAID GLAN CONWY
St Clair	ST CLEARS
St CleEr	ST CLEARS
St George	LLANSANFFRAID GLAN CONWY
St Winifred's Well	HOLYWELL
Strata Florida	YSTRADGYNLAIS
Suck	ABER-SOCH
Swillies	LLANFAIR PWLLGWYNGYLL
Swydd y Waun	CHIRK

Swys	CAERSŴS
Sychan	ABERSYCHAN, BLAENAVON
Sychdyn	BROUGHTON
Table Mountain	CRUCYWEL
Taf	CARDIFF
Tamar	CARDIFF
Tame	CARDIFF
Tawe	CARDIFF, CLYDACH, PONTARDAWE, SWANSEA
Teifi	CARDIGAN, LLANDDEWI BREFI
Teleri	ABERTYLERI
Thames	CARDIFF
Thaw	COWBRIDGE
Ton-du	TONYPANDY
Tongwynlais	TONYPANDY
Tonpentre	TONYPANDY
Ton-teg	TONYPANDY
Towy	LLANYMDDYFRI
Towyn	TYWYN
Tonyrefail	TONYPANDY
Traeth Bach	PENRHYNDEUDRAETH
Traeth Coch	PENTRAETH
Traeth Mawr	PENRHYNDEUDRAETII, PORTHMADOG
Trallwm	TRALLWNG
Traws(y)bryn	TRAWSFYNYDD
Tredelerch	RHYMNI
Trefddyn	PONT-Y-PŴL
Tregeiriog	LLANSANFFRAID GLYNCEIRIOG
Treharris	BARGOED
Tremadog	PORTHMADOG
Trevethin	PONT-Y-PŴL
Trewalchmai	GWALCHMAI
Tryfan	RHOSTRYFAN
Tŷ Gwyn	WHITLAND

Twrch	ABER-SOCH
Tyddyn y Benllech	BENLLECH
Venta Belgarum	CAER-WENT
Venta Silurum	CAER-WENT, CHEPSTOW
Welsh Frankton	WELSHPOOL
Wnion	DOLGELLAU
Wye	HAY-ON-WYE
Wygyr	CEMAES
Wysg	CAERLEON, USK
Y Glais	DOWLAIS
Ynys Bŷr	MAENORBŶR
Ynys Geti	CILGETI
Ynys Gorad Goch	LLANFAIR PWLLGWYNGYLL
Ynys Gybi	HOLYHEAD
Ynys Tysilio	LLANFAIR PWLLGWYNGYLL
Ynys y Barri	BARRI
Ynys-wen	ABER-CRAF
Yr Eifl	CAERNARFON
Ystwyth	ABERYSTWYTH